The Power to Learn

TITLES OF RELATED INTEREST

The Wadsworth College Success_SM_ Series

Right from the Start: Managing Your Way to College Success
by Robert Holkeboer (1993)

*Integrating College Study Skills: Reasoning in Reading, Listening,
and Writing*, Third Edition, by Peter Elias Sotiriou (1993)

*The Mountain Is High Unless You Take the Elevator:
Success Strategies for Adult Learners* by Laurence N. Smith
and Timothy L. Walter (1992)

Mastering Mathematics: How to Be a Great Math Student
by Richard Manning Smith (1991)

Merlin: The Sorcerer's Guide to Survival in College
by Christopher F. Monte (1990)

The Freshman Year Experience_SM_ Series

Your College Experience: Strategies for Success, Concise
Edition, by A. Jerome Jewler and John N. Gardner,
with Mary-Jane McCarthy (1993)

Your College Experience: Strategies for Success by John N. Gardner
and A. Jerome Jewler (1992)

College Is Only the Beginning, Second Edition, by John N. Gardner
and A. Jerome Jewler (1989)

Create Your College Success by Robert A. Friday (1988)

Step by Step to College Success by A. Jerome Jewler
and John N. Gardner (1987)

The Power to Learn

Helping Yourself to College Success

William E. Campbell

University of Wisconsin–River Falls

Wadsworth Publishing Company
Belmont, California
A Division of Wadsworth, Inc.

To Susan and Jason

Wadsworth College Success Series Editor: Angela Gantner
Editorial Assistant: Tricia Schumacher
Production Editor: Jerilyn Emori
Text and Cover Designer: Ann Butler
Print Buyer: Randy Hurst
Art Editor: Nancy Spellman
Permissions Editor: Jeanne Bosschart
Copy Editor: Judith Hibbard
Illustrators: Carole Lawson and Nancy Spellman
Cover Illustrator: Stearney Design Group
Signing Representative: Cathy Twiss-Weil
Compositor: TBH/Typecast, Inc.
Printer: Malloy Lithographing, Inc.

 This book is printed on acid-free paper.

Printed in the United States of America

1 2 3 4 5 6 7 8 9 10 — 97 96 95 94 93

Library of Congress Cataloging-in-Publication Data

Campbell, William E.
    The power to learn : helping yourself to college success / William E. Campbell
        p.   cm.
    Includes index.
    ISBN 0-534-19404-4
    1. College student orientation—United States.   2. Study,   Method of.   I. Title.
    LB2343.32.C36   1993
    378.1'702812—dc20
                                                                    92-20015

Brief Contents

●--------------→

Contents

Chapter 8

Learning Through Reading 115

Chapter 9

Learning Through Experience 133

Preface

TO THE INSTRUCTOR

There was a time, our elders tell us, when students came to college thoroughly prepared to do college level work. They could read and analyze texts, write coherent essays, master calculus, work independently in laboratories, and engage in stimulating, intellectual conversations. I'm skeptical of those tales—I suspect we all tend to remember the students we wanted to be—but there is no doubt that many freshmen entering college today do not know how to succeed in college.

Why not? For many reasons: More people go to college; high schools are not as academic as they once were; popular culture commands more of the time and attention of young people; admissions standards have changed. For one reason or another, many students have no reason to learn the skills good students practice until they reach college.

As a result, many colleges and universities have created special programs to help students learn those skills. These programs take many forms: freshman seminars, survival skills courses, extended orientation sessions, summer precollege camps, and so on. *The Power to Learn: Helping Yourself to College Success* is designed for these programs. It can be used as a text for survival skills courses and freshman seminars modeled on John Gardner's University 101. It can be used as a guide for orientation sessions or as secondary reading for precollege programs. It can be used as a supplement to any content-based course that requires freshmen to study in ways they have not studied before—calculus, philosophy, history of ideas, biology. It can be used as recommended reading for freshmen.

Part I will help students learn the basics: setting goals for themselves, managing their time, attacking their courses, integrating their classes with the rest of their lives, learning with others, and using their memories. Part II teaches the skills successful students use in specific courses. Some courses transmit information by lecture, requiring listening and note-taking skills. Some courses require large amounts of reading; to succeed, students must not only read the material but must record and remember the crucial information as well. Some courses depend on direct experience; for example, laboratories, internships, fieldwork. Students must learn how to internalize these experiences. Some courses require practice; for example, mathematics, accounting, composition, foreign language. Students need to know how to integrate their practice with their coursework.

Part III makes the general ideas of Parts I and II particular. It presents case studies of eight students experiencing some of the difficulties that typically beset freshmen who are learning to cope with college. Some instructors, in some contexts, may wish to begin with Part III.

The basic strategy of this book is to empower the student. In recent years a variety of pedagogical movements has swept through undergraduate education, promising to make learning more effective, more efficient, more fun: the active learning movement, the critical thinking movement, the collaborative learning movement, the basic skills movement, the learning styles movement, the writing-across-the-curriculum movement, the case studies movement, and so on. All have been effective, in their own ways. But none of them has become pervasive. Consequently, most students are taught just as their instructors were taught, through lectures and readings and demonstrations that do little to engage them in their courses. This book is meant to teach students ways to engage themselves in their coursework, no matter how they are taught.

Many of the methods this book teaches parallel the methods of these various pedagogical movements. The book demonstrates ways in which students can become actively engaged in even the largest mass lectures; how they can think critically, through writing and speaking, in all of their courses; how they can learn collaboratively even if their instructors do not encourage collaboration; how they can develop their basic skills and investigate their own learning styles independently of whatever their instructors do in the classroom; how they can learn through writing across their own curricula; how they can study their own cases.

However you use this book, I encourage you to encourage your students to do the exercises. Reading about studying is about as effective as lecturing about studying. No matter how true readings (or lectures) might be, they mean little unless they are put to work. And I encourage you to invent your own exercises to go along with this text. Tie them to the particulars of the course you are teaching or to the other courses your students are taking. The more exercises your students complete, the more engaged they will be in your course—and the more they will learn.

Acknowledgments Many persons have helped me write this book. I wish to thank the following reviewers for their suggestions and comments: Harley F. Anton, Middle Tennessee State University; Rose Baugh, Georgia College; Joanne E. Fowler, Kennesaw State College; Rebecca Leonard, North Carolina State University; Judi M. Roller, Wright State University; Susan Schaefer, University of California, Irvine; Kathleen Shipley, California State University, Stanislaus; Greg Smith, University of Wisconsin Center, Rock County; and Margaret Turner, Coppin State College. My thanks also go to my colleagues and friends Faith Gabelnick, Peter Whelan, Van Gooch, Beth Carlson, Karla Stacey, Lee Goodhart, Charles Braithwaite, Dawn Braithwaite, John Buchl, Joan Reicosky, Tom Turner, and Mike Reich for sharing their wisdom; to Toby Fulwiler for teaching me about journals; and to the thousands of students at the University of Wisconsin–LaCrosse, University of Minnesota, Morris, and University of Wisconsin–River Falls who have taught me how they learn.

TO THE STUDENT

The Power to Learn: Helping Yourself to College Success is meant for college freshmen. *All* freshmen: jocks, brains, returning adults, grinds, frat rats and sorority sisters, nat-scis and comp-scis, couch potatoes, minority students, majority students, and everyone else. Despite your many differences, all of you have one thing in common. You are entering a new world, a complex world, a world with few familiar signposts. *The Power to Learn* will help you navigate through this new world.

Over the past 20 years I have worked with thousands and thousands of freshmen. I have taught them, advised them, and invented precollege and tutoring and honors programs for them. I have seen most of them succeed and some of them fail. During those years I have learned a few things about success and failure in college.

One of the most important lessons I have learned is that almost everyone can succeed in college. Of all the students I have known, few were not smart enough to make it in college. That doesn't mean that everyone can succeed everywhere, of course. Colleges differ widely in their expectations of freshmen, just as freshmen differ widely in their levels of ambition and preparation. So the first task is to find a college whose expectations match your ambition and preparation. I assume that you have already done that.

I also assume that you have already committed yourself to succeeding. I have learned—the hard way—that nothing I say, nothing your instructors say, nothing your advisor or coach or even your parents say, can motivate you to succeed in college. You must find that motivation within yourself. The good news is once you have that motivation, once you are committed to doing whatever you must do to succeed, you can do it. *The Power to Learn* will show you how.

This is not a recipe book. It will not lay out for you a daily schedule, it will not prescribe a single method of taking notes or studying for tests, and it will not tell you how you have to live your life. But *The Power to Learn* will tell you the principles successful students use, and it will show you a variety of ways you might put those principles to work. If you have enrolled in a college that is appropriate for you and if you are committed to the task, these principles will show you how to succeed.

The Power to Learn consists of three parts. Part I is devoted to general principles: setting your goals, managing your time and arranging your life, attacking your coursework, taking advantage of your memory, and so on. Part II is devoted to the specifics of studying: taking notes, reading texts, and the techniques students use to succeed in various sorts of courses. Part III tells the stories of eight students who have gone through many of the typical freshman travails.

You need not read this book in sequence. If you are desperate to know how to get the most out of your reading, start with Chapter 7. If you are anxious for some models to follow, skip to Part III and find a student like yourself. One of the most basic general principles this book will teach you is to use whatever method of study works for you. Apply that principle as you read this book: Use it in whatever way it helps you.

Enjoy your journey.

Preliminaries

Many students think that succeeding in college is a matter of using the right study methods. "If I can just figure out how to remember all this stuff, I'll do fine on the test," they tell me. "If I only knew how to get started on this paper, the rest would come easily." "If I could just read faster, I could get all of my studying done in plenty of time." **I**t's not that simple. Sure, in order to succeed you must remember lots of material, you must get a good start on your papers, and you must read your textbooks efficiently. This book will help you learn how to do all of those things—eventually. But the first thing you must do in order to succeed in college is decide that you want to succeed and what will count as success. Chapter 1 will help you do that. **C**hapter Two will help you decide how you're going to balance the various demands on your time. Chapter 3 will help you understand a few basic principles for succeeding in your courses.

Chapter 4 will show you how to integrate your extracurricular activities into your life. Chapter 5 will demonstrate the value of learning with your colleagues and peers. Finally, Chapter 6 will tell you a little about how your memory works and how you can use it to your best advantage. **O**nce you understand these preliminaries we can turn to Part II, which deals with the specific study skills you'll need to succeed in college.

1

Creating Your Own Success

This chapter argues that you have the opportunity to make yourself up in any way you choose when you begin your college career. The first step is to decide what sort of student you want to be. In order to do that you must be aware of why you are going to college, and you need to focus on some long-range, mid-range, and short-range goals. And then you must commit yourself to reaching those goals by engaging in the activities that lead to them.

Sounds easy, doesn't it? Well, it's not quite that easy. But if you complete the exercises in this chapter, you'll have a good start.

Choosing to Succeed

Are you as smart as you would like to be? As athletic? As good-looking? Few of us are. But most of us can't do anything about it. Even if we could become brilliant, gorgeous Olympians overnight, we would still be stuck in the same routines we follow daily. Our families, friends, and coworkers might admire the changes, but they would still treat us in the same way they do now. Our daily chores would be the same, so our new brilliance, strength, and beauty would not do us much good. In short, even if we change, our environment will remain the same.

But if you are about to start college, you are changing your environment. Few people will know you, and your daily routine will be brand new. So you have a chance to make yourself up any way you would like. You could decide to be more athletic than you have ever been, for instance. Would that make you a better athlete? It could. Devoting more time and energy to football or tennis or aerobic dance than you used to will result in better athletic performance. Or you could decide to be better looking; if you spend more time and energy on your appearance, it will improve.

And you can decide to be a better student than you have ever been. Will that really make you a better student? It could. If you spend more time and energy on your schoolwork than you have ever spent before, you will learn more than you ever have, and your grades will improve accordingly.

The point is, *you* get to choose what sort of student you will be in college. You have probably never had that opportunity before. When you started grade school you weren't even aware of what choice is, let alone able to exercise it. And the rest of your school career just followed along. You couldn't even choose whether or not you would go to school until you turned 16—you had to go, by law. And even at 16 your choices were probably severely limited by your parents. Sure, you made lots of individual choices along the way. You chose the college prep or the vocational track, you chose to go out for sports or to be a brain, you chose to spend your time studying or socializing. But you probably made few of those choices consciously. Most high school students make their choices reflexively, by doing what their friends do or what their teachers say they should do or what their parents say they must do.

Sometimes new freshmen tell me that they never really wanted to go to college; they just sort of ended up here because their parents expected it, because all their friends were going, or because there were no other choices. I tell them that they are in serious trouble. Life in college is so demanding—academically, socially, personally—that they will probably have great difficulty succeeding unless they can make some sort of commitment to the task.

Students who are starting college after being out of high school for a few years have already made the most significant choice: to go back to school. Sometimes that choice is forced by economic conditions ("I can't get a decent job without a degree"), by changes in family situations ("my spouse divorced me, and I need to change my life"), or by a new interest in academics ("I decided I want to learn more about my heritage"). Still, choosing to become a freshman who is several years older than the norm takes some conscious thought and some nerve.

No matter what sort of freshman you are—18-year-old just out of high school, returning adult, absolutely determined engineer-to-be, or whatever—you have some serious choices to make. The first one is, what kind of student will you be? None of your professors know you. If you appear to them to be a successful student, they will assume that you *are* a successful student and will treat you accordingly.

It's not quite as simple as that, of course. Choosing to be a successful student means nothing unless you convert your choice into actions. But the first step is to decide what sort of student you want to be. And to do that you need to set some goals for yourself.

Setting Goals

There's an old saying in career-counseling offices: If you don't know where you're going, you'll wind up somewhere else. The first step in deciding what sort of student you want to be is to decide where you are headed.

Many of you have already mapped out your lives: go to college, go to law school, become a corporate attorney, have a family, be president of a company, retire to Arizona, die. Many of you have not. Don't worry about it. Making plans for your life after college is a good idea, but far from crucial. You'll probably change careers four or five times during your lifetime, no matter what plans you make today.

Setting some goals for your college career *is* crucial. You should have a fairly clear idea of why you are in college. Be honest with yourself; your true reasons may differ from what you told the admissions counselor or your parents or your spouse. Some students come to college to get a good job after they graduate, some to satisfy their parents, some to scratch a burning itch to know more, some to party for 4 years on someone else's nickel, some to become educated persons, some for all of these reasons and more. Each of these reasons is as valid as any other. But you should know what your reasons for coming to college are.

EXERCISE 1.1

Find or buy a small notebook to use as a journal to accompany this book. Loose-leaf notebooks work the best; they allow you to add pages where necessary, take pages out to use elsewhere, and so on. But spiral-bound notebooks will work also. Use your journal for writing the exercises that appear in these pages, for writing reactions to what you read in this book, for writing specific study plans for yourself based on the general suggestions you find, and so on.

Writing in your journal will help you think about what you are reading and remember it. And writing in your journal will help you translate what you are learning into specific courses of action. If you find it a helpful supplement to this book, keep a journal to accompany your textbooks and your classes.

Now for the first exercise: In your journal, write the reasons why you are going to college. Begin on a clean sheet of paper, and put the date, the time, and a title ("Why I Am Going to College") at the top. Write for 10 minutes without stopping; that way you will write as you think, you will think as you write, and your writing will stimulate your thoughts. Don't worry about the mechanics of writing—punctuation, capitalization, paragraphs, sentence structure, and so on. Your journal is like a diary. You write it to yourself, so the regular rules of writing don't count as long as you can understand what you write.

Be honest with yourself. Your high school counselor will never see what you write, nor will your family, nor your professors. If you came to college to have a good time, to become a famous writer, to get ready for the NFL, or to find a spouse, write that down. And write down all of the other reasons why you came to college. Most students have at least three or four; many can list ten or fifteen.

When you have completed your writing, read it over. Anything to add? Add it.

LONG-RANGE GOALS

Once you are conscious of your reasons for coming to college, you can begin setting some goals. First, long-range goals. Long-range goals are the things you hope to achieve during your college career: getting into law school, learning as much as you can about a particular subject, having as much fun as possible while earning a usable degree, becoming intellectually well-rounded, or making varsity. Once again, you must be honest with yourself. You may tell everyone that your number one goal is to get into law school when actually you are much more interested in becoming the best gymnast you can be, or learning to write novels, or partying around the clock. It's okay, in some circumstances, to deceive—none of us is completely honest with everyone all of the time—but don't deceive yourself. You must know what your goals are.

EXERCISE 1.2

First, reread your first journal entry ("Why I Am Going to College"). Does it still seem correct? Complete? If not, add whatever you must to make it correct or complete.

Now, on a clean sheet of paper (don't forget your heading: date, time, title), list everything you hope to get out of your college career. Hold nothing back; include economic benefits, knowledge and skills, fun, relationships, and anything else you can think of. Most students can generate at least six or eight things; many come up with more than twenty-five. Now rank-order these benefits by writing a "1" next to the one that is most important to you, a "2" next to the second most important, and so on. Finally, cross out all but numbers 1, 2, and 3. Those are your three most important reasons for going to college: your long-range goals.

MID- AND SHORT-RANGE GOALS

If your number one long-range goal is to get into law school, then your mid-range goals should be to maintain a law-school-acceptable grade point average, cultivate some professors who will write you good letters of recommendation, and major in something that will impress the admissions committee. Your short-range goals should be to earn an A on your next exam and converse with one of your professors in her* office.

If your number one goal is making the varsity, then your mid-range goals should involve lots of practice time and at least enough schoolwork to keep you eligible. Your short-term goals should be to gain coach's approval in practice every day and earn at least Cs on your next exams.

━━━━━━━━▶ EXERCISE 1.3 ◀━━━━━━━━

On the top of a clean sheet of paper in your journal, write the first of your long-range goals from Exercise 1.2. Now list all of the things you can do during your college career that will contribute to reaching that goal. (If you don't know, guess. But make it a point to find out later how accurate your guess is.) Don't be shy; write down everything you can think of that might contribute. Once again, rank-order your entries in order of importance by numbering them. Cross out all but the top five. Repeat this process for your second and third reasons for going to college. These are your mid-range goals for your college career.

For each of these mid-range goals—you should have fifteen—write two things you can do during this semester or quarter to help you achieve it. (I know, you're running out of space on your paper. Write small, write in the margins, write between the lines; it's good practice for taking notes in class.) These are your short-range goals, goals you can work toward immediately.

Once you have completed these goal-setting exercises, you might go through them again with those people who will share in your college experience: your parents, your spouse, your children. Have each person go through the same steps from your perspective: the reasons

---

*A note about pronouns: Current English usage lacks a tidy convention for gender-free pronouns. "Him/her" and "s/he" are clumsy; "they" is misleading. Consequently, in this book I simply alternate between male and female pronouns.

why *you* are going to college, the goals that follow for *you*, and so on. Finally, compare notes; you may be amazed at the differences between the lists. (Note: This exercise can be threatening to parents. Treat them gently.)

Remember that all of these goals are equally valid. Because you are the one who chose to go to college, you have the right to set your own goals. They may not be goals you'd care to share with your high school counselor, who thinks you're going to become an astrophysicist, or with your current instructors, who want you to major in whatever discipline they teach. You may even have a hard time admitting to yourself what your real goals are. Who wants to confess that the primary goal for running track is to wear that nifty sweatsuit, or that the first goal in a history course is to find an excuse to talk to that sexy sophomore? But if you don't confess your real goals to yourself, or if you're not aware of your reasons for going to college, your life for the next few years will be a constant struggle. You'll be going in two or three directions at once and not getting anywhere.

Of course if you're not paying for your college education yourself, you may have to negotiate your goals with whomever is footing the bill. But remember that you are investing your time and effort in this endeavor. That makes you a partner in the deal.

Your reasons for going to college and the goals you set accordingly will change. They have probably changed at least once since you arrived on campus and realized that calculus is really hard, or that philosophy is not just talk. No problem. We all change our reasons for what we do, and the goals we are working toward change accordingly. Or we discover that our goals are unrealistic, for some reason or other, and we change directions. Just make sure that your own goals are consistent with your reasons for being in college. Don't keep thinking you're going to be an engineer when you know you can't, or won't, do calculus. Or don't stay with your philosophy major even though you absolutely hate your philosophy courses.

Every few months you should repeat the goal-setting exercises in your journal. Even if you think you know where you are headed and exactly how you're going to get there, writing about your goals will help you. As you're writing, you'll think of some new short-range goals that will contribute, or you'll think of an alternative path to your long-range goal, or you might even discover that an entirely different reason for going to college is emerging. If that happens to you, make sure you change your goals to match.

Being conscious of why you are going to college and translating those reasons into specific goals give your college years meaning.

With goals in mind you have something to work toward, something to achieve; you are no longer simply putting in time, the way most of us spent our high school years.

You probably know some students who have no goals. They tend to sit around a lot, watching the soaps, going out nights, avoiding their homework. They tend to be very unhappy. They tend to drop out, or stop out, or flunk out of school.

Becoming an Active Student

Okay, now you have set some goals for yourself. You know where you are headed—your long-range goals—and you know at least some of what you will have to do to get there—your mid- and short-range goals. In setting those goals, you have chosen what sort of student you want to be. What next?

Now you have to work to meet your goals. That's easy for me to say, but not so easy for you to do. Keep in mind that *you* made the choices, *you* set the goals. If they really reflect what you want, you should be able to keep working toward them. If, on the other hand, at some point your goals seem unattainable or irrelevant to your life, you need to rethink them.

But how do you do it? By leaping in, by throwing yourself into attaining your short-term goals, by committing yourself to reaching the goals you have set for yourself. Ever play basketball? Or tennis, football, chess, or any other game? Then you should already know the value of throwing yourself into an activity. In basketball, the worst thing you can do is stand around. When you stand around, nothing happens—except every now and then the ball bounces off your head. It's the same in tennis. If all you do is react to your opponent's game, you are under his control, and you are likely to lose your match. In football, if you do not actively engage yourself in the game, you get clobbered. In chess, if you lose track of the continuity of the moves, you're finished.

In order to succeed in sports and games you must leap in; you must actively work toward the tasks at hand, and you must concentrate. The same principle holds with going to college. Suppose your long-range goal is to go to law school. You and your advisor have already settled upon a good schedule for a prelaw student. What next? Remember that in order to get into law school you must have a good grade point average; that was one of your mid-range goals. That means you'll have to study fairly hard. You also will need some good recommendations. Therefore you should get to know your professors on a personal basis. And you should be able to list responsible positions in student activities on your application, so you should join some clubs or organizations on campus.

Suppose your long-range goal is to learn all you possibly can about a particular subject—anthropology. You have signed up for Introduction to Cultural Anthropology, the only anthropology course your advisor would let you take. What else can you do? Work extremely hard at that course. Go to every film and lecture your anthropology instructor recommends, and read every book she mentions. Join the Anthropology Club, if there is one. Volunteer to assist with your professor's research. Get to know the secretary of the anthropology department. Hang around with anthropology majors.

Suppose your goal is to make yourself more employable. You've already declared a business major, and your advisor has started you out with Accounting I, Introduction to Business Law, and some general education courses. What else can you do? Find a part-time job that will show you how businesses work. Volunteer to be the treasurer of the organizations you belong to. Join the business fraternity. Start looking for internship opportunities.

Suppose your goal is to be a varsity football player. You've gone out for the team, and you're doing okay so far. What else can you do? Study enough to pass your courses, at least; you can't make varsity if you're not eligible. Let the coaches know your ambition, and follow their advice. Spend a lot of time in the weight room.

EXERCISE 1.4

In your journal, turn to the page that lists your short- and mid-range goals. For each of your short-range goals, write one specific action you can undertake that will help you achieve it.

Whatever your goals might be, you will never reach them if you sit around waiting for good things to happen to you. You have to make them happen. You have to become actively engaged in pursuing your goals. Various studies indicate that the freshmen at the highest risk of failing in college are those who do not become actively involved in some aspect of college life. They live off campus and miss out on the activities of the residence halls. Or they don't go to class. Or they fail to get to know anyone.

In order to succeed, you must get actively involved in something. And, now that you have set some goals for yourself, you should have a clear idea of what you should get involved in.

EXERCISE 1.5

In your journal, write for 10 minutes on the most important lessons you have learned from this chapter.

Summary

In this chapter I have tried to convince you that you have the opportunity to create yourself anew when you start college. To create yourself consciously, you must determine why you are going to college and use that insight to set some goals for yourself. You must turn your goals into specific activities. And finally, you must leap into those activities; you must actively engage yourself in your tasks.

2

Managing Your Time

➤ **Y**our life as a college student will be different from whatever you have known before. You will be under considerable pressure to perform, and your work will be held to higher standards than you may have seen previously. At the same time you will be presented with a wide range of distractions. You must decide when to work and when to be distracted. You must manage your time.

Time management is one of the most difficult tasks freshmen face. College life offers more choices than most freshmen are used to seeing. If you are a recent high school graduate, you are used to having most of your time managed for you. Be in this class at this hour, that class at that hour, go to lunch at 12:20, go to practice at 3:10, dinner at 6:30, work at 8. But in college you have fewer classes to go to, with large blocks of free time between them. There are no teachers or study hall monitors or parents hanging over you, threatening you with severe bodily harm if you don't do your homework. Furthermore, there are countless distractors: new friends who want to visit, expeditions setting off for downtown, sports and games, TV and movies. Many freshmen find the choices exhilarating and their new freedom absolutely intoxicating.

If you are an adult returning to college after having been out of school for some years, you may also have difficulty managing your time—but for different reasons. After years of employment or homemaking, most returning adults are used to fairly rigid, demanding schedules with timely rewards and punishments. If you are late for work 3 days in a row, you suffer immediately. If you fail to feed the kids, they let you know instantly. But in college, the schedule is more flexible and the rewards and punishments are deferred. If you are late for class, nothing is likely to happen. If you don't get your assignment in on time, no one is going to complain. Of course, in both cases your grade is likely to suffer. But that doesn't happen until the end of the quarter. And so you may decide that the immediate demands of home or job take precedence over the deferred demands of your classes.

All students talk about managing their time better. "Boy, am I behind" is a complaint frequently heard in the Union or the dorm or the library; "Tomorrow I'm really going to get organized." But intending to get organized isn't good enough. You have to do something about it. This chapter will show you how.

Weekly Schedules

The best way to manage your time is with a weekly schedule. First, reread your journal entries from Chapter 1 to remind yourself of why you are going to college and what your goals are. Are those entries still accurate? If not, bring them up to date with a new entry.

Second, write a preliminary schedule. On a blank sheet of full-sized paper, make a grid like the one in Figure 2.1. Use a pen; this part is permanent. Across the top write the days of the week, Monday through Sunday. Down the left-hand margin write the hours of the day, starting with when you plan to get up and ending with when you plan to go to bed. Next, write in all of your fixed commitments: your classes, your job if you have one, football or choir or play practice, meals. These are the things that are already scheduled for you or to which you have already committed yourself.

There should be lots of blank boxes left over. Those blank boxes represent time that is free and uncommitted. Fill them in. Use a pencil for this part so you can switch things around later. Your goals from Chapter 1 should determine how you fill in the blanks. If your long-range goal is to get into law school, and your mid- and short-range goals include getting good grades, getting to know your professors, and being active in campus activities, then your schedule should reflect those goals. "Study" should fill much of the blank space, with some entries for club and committee meetings and socializing with faculty. If your primary goal is to play varsity football, your schedule should include some study—you have to stay eligible, remember— with large blocks of time for practice, weights, and taking care of the requirements of your body.

Figure 2.1 shows the schedule of a freshman whose goal is to make herself more employable through a business major and an off-campus job selling clothes. Notice that she has boxed in all of the times she plans to study, so they are plainly visible. She has four 3-credit-hour courses, so she spends 12 hours in class each week. She has decided to get good grades, so she has scheduled 31 hours of study per week. She has also scheduled some time for exercise, for leisure, for relaxation, and for housekeeping chores. Sunday mornings and afternoons are flexible; she can do her housekeeping then, or she can study if she has an exam coming up or a large project to complete.

Figure 2.2 is the schedule her boyfriend designed for himself. He is also a freshman, not quite as ambitious, and undecided about his major field. He is taking four 3-credit-hour courses as well, plus a 1-credit-hour lab—13 credit hours in all. Sunday afternoon football, late night TV, and going out on Friday and Saturday nights are important to him, so he has built those activities into his schedule. He has also left Saturdays open for doing whatever he feels like doing.

Figure 2.3 is the schedule of a single mom who works 25–30 hours a week selling real estate. Her two kids, 9 and 11, are in school, and her mother takes care of them afternoons. They spend most weekends with her ex-husband; that's when she works her heaviest hours. She also works three afternoons a week and the occasional evening when she has a hot prospect. She's working toward a degree in social work, but her job comes first. Without it, she couldn't go to school at all.

She signed up for four courses, but during the first week she could see that her schedule was impossible. She dropped chemistry—the labs just took too much time—and decided to concentrate on the remaining three. Her adviser warned her that she was probably sentencing herself to a 5- or 6-year program. "Better than no program at all," she replied. She tries to study about 30 hours a week, depending on whether she has to work in the evening. She does her calculus problems during the day, when she can hide in the library. Evenings she reads as much of her sociology and economics as she can handle while she helps the kids with their homework, oversees their TV, negotiates their disagreements, and gets them to bed. Once or twice a month she steals a Saturday night or Sunday morning to catch up.

Figure 2.1 *Sample schedule: freshman business major*

	Mon	Tues	Wed	Thurs	Fri	Sat	Sun
8-9	Bkfst	Bkfst	Bkfst	Bkfst	Bkfst	SLE	EP!
9-10	Accounting 101		Acct 101		Acct 101		Church
10-11	Accounting problems	Eng 102	Study Acct	Eng 102	Study Acct	Work	Laundry,
11-12		Read Eng		Read Eng			shopping, chores,
12-1	Lunch	Lunch	Lunch	Lunch	Lunch		study
1-2	Math 220	Work	Math 220	Work	Math 220		
2-3	Study Math		Study Math		Study Math		
3-4	Business 100-Intro		Business 100		Business 100		
4-5	Exercise ———→				Exercise ———→		
5-6	Dinner, ———→				Dinner, relax ———→		
6-7	relax ———————————————————→						
7-8					Go out w/friends	?	
8-9	S T U D Y !					?	S T U D Y !
9-10						?	
10-11						?	
11-12						?	

Figure 2.2 *Sample schedule: freshman undecided major*

	Mon	Tues	Wed	Thurs	Fri	Sat	Sun
7-8	Get up, bkfst	→					
8-9	Read	Engl	Read	Engl	Read	Play	
9-10	Philosophy 200	101	Phil 200	101	Phil 200		
10-11	Read	→					
11-12	Spanish 103		Span 103		Span 103		
12-1	Lunch	→					
1-2	Chores, TV,	Write letters,	relax	→			Watch football
2-3	Biology 100	↓	Bio 100	↓	Bio 100		
3-4	Study	Bio lab	Work—Study Job—Admissions				
4-5							
5-6	↓	↓	↓	↓	↓	↓	↓
6-7	Dinner	→					
7-8	STUDY				R U N		STUDY
8-9					↓	↓	
9-10							↓
10-11	TV	→					

Figure 2.3 *Sample schedule: single mother*

	Mon	Tues	Wed	Thurs	Fri	Sat	Sun
7-8	Kids to school →					SLEEP!	
8-9	Dishes, laundry, pickup,						
9-10	get ready for school →					Work	
10-11	Economics 101	Study	Econ 101	Study	Econ 101		
11-12	Math 210		Math 210		Math 210		
12-1	Work		Work		Work		
1-2		Sociology 100		Soc 100			
2-3		Study		Study			
3-4							
4-5							
5-6	Pick up kids, dinner, homework					Personal Time	Family
6-7	Laundry, etc. →						
7-8	Study / family →						
8-9	Study / family →						
9-10	Study / family →						
10-11	Study / family →						

These students used the following basic principles as they filled in their schedules. You should follow them too.

THE TWO-FOR-ONE RULE

No matter what your goals are, studying will be one of the crucial entries in your schedule. How much should you study? It depends on your level of ambition, your level of ability, and the level of difficulty of the courses you are taking, of course. But there is a basic rule of thumb. Most colleges and universities expect you to study at least 2 hours for every hour you spend in class. If your goals include high grades, if studying effectively takes you a long time, or if you are taking extremely demanding courses, you should allow more than 2 hours per hour spent in class. If grades are not high on your priority list, if you are a quick study, or if your courses are not unduly demanding, less than two hours will do.

Note that the business major's schedule in Figure 2.1 shows 31 hours of study for 12 hours in class. She knows herself and her courses well enough to know that she must spend that much time studying to earn the grades she needs to meet her goals. Her boyfriend's schedule is less rigorous. He is carrying 13 credit-hours and plans to spend 26 hours studying—two-for-one exactly.* The single mother majoring in social work plans to study about 20 hours for 9 credits. Sometimes she will have to use family time to catch up.

Studying means more than simply doing your homework. Homework is what your instructor assigns—chapters to read, problem sets to solve, papers to write. Studying is all of that, plus a lot more—reviewing your class notes, inventing possible questions for next week's exam, reading background material, preparing for tomorrow's quiz. You will find that simply doing your homework will produce mediocre grades. In order to do well in college, you have to do more than just what your instructors assign—you have to study.

WHEN TO STUDY

When you were in high school, you probably did your homework at night. In college, that is probably the worst time to study. Most people

----

*Labs don't fit well into the two-for-one formula, because the work you are doing in the laboratory is meant to supplement what you are learning in the lecture portion of the course. Studio art courses, PE courses, and music courses in which you perform fall into the same category. Use credit-hours as the basis for figuring your study time.

are most alert in the morning, somewhat less alert in the afternoon, and least alert in the evening. So for most people the evening is the worst time of day to learn anything. In high school, you did most of your learning in class; homework was supplemental. But in college, most of what you learn will come from your studying, not from class. Consequently, you should do as much studying as you can early in the day.

Make a practice of using the time between classes to study. Don't bother going home. That takes too much time, and you are likely to get distracted into a conversation along the way. Use the library, an empty classroom, a corner of a hallway, or the Union. You will find that the hour you have free between College Algebra and Accounting is a great time to study. Use it to work tomorrow's algebra problems, while today's lesson is fresh in your mind.

If you do most of your studying during the day, you will have at least some free time left in the evening. You can participate in intramurals, do your laundry, go to movies, watch TV, visit with your spouse or friends, and still be virtuous—you've already done your studying for the day.

GO TO CLASS

If you haven't started college yet, you may find this section ridiculous. Of course you should go to class, and you will, too. But if you have already started college, you know that the rules are much looser than they were in high school. Only a few professors take attendance, and the ones who do only mutter to themselves. They don't seem to punish the students who are not present, so cutting class is easy. And it's tempting, too, with so many distractors pulling you in every direction.

So why should you go to class? Because that's what you came to college for, that's why. Your very first journal entry was on your reasons for coming to college; remember what they were? I guarantee you that, whatever those reasons were, they involve succeeding in your classes (by your own definition of success).

It's true that, in most classes, nothing terrible will seem to happen to you if you miss a class. But appearances can be deceiving. Some instructors factor attendance into the final grade, even though they never mention it. (Is that fair? Perhaps not, but there's nothing you can do about it, so don't spend any time being angry.)

On the other hand, some instructors genuinely don't care if you come to class or not. Go to class anyway. No matter what sort of instructors you have, the real penalty for skipping class is severe: You will have no notion of what went on. Instructors write their tests on what they think is important. They also write their lectures on what they think is important. Going to class is the best way to find out what the instructor thinks is important, and therefore what will be on the test.

There will be times when you must skip a class: You are in the hospital, or the team you are on is going to East Podunk for a tournament, or your child is sick, or you need to finish the giant project due in the next hour. Some of those absences will be excused, some will not. In either case, do whatever you have to do to find out what went on in class. Ask your instructor. (But *don't* ask, "Did anything go on in class?" She will be offended. Ask instead, "I missed yesterday's lecture; could you summarize the high points for me?") Ask a classmate, and borrow his notes. (But don't think that someone else's notes are a substitute for your own; they are not.) Skipping class is always a trade-off. You gain the time, but you lose the knowledge you would have gained. It's seldom a good trade.

OUT-OF-CLASS ACTIVITIES

Freshmen frequently fill every blank space in their schedules with "study." Don't do it. You will probably not follow such a schedule, no matter how strong your resolve. But even if you could, you should not. College offers you much more than an opportunity to earn grades and a degree. There are concerts, art shows, exhibitions; lectures, sports events, colloquia; films, receptions, mixers. Take advantage of these opportunities. You will meet a lot of new people, you will have a good time (mostly), and you will learn a lot. Furthermore, what you learn in these extracurricular events will add to what you are learning in your classes.

So build some activities into your weekly schedule. Consult the campus newspaper to see what's coming up. Pick one event that you know you will enjoy and one that is completely beyond your experience. The business major whose schedule appears in Figure 2.1 frequently goes to films or concerts on Friday and Saturday nights, but never does anything but study during the week. Her boyfriend, however, is less rigid. He is willing to give up study time on weeknights to go to the occasional event—but he makes up that study time on weekends.

The single mother whose schedule is shown in Figure 2.3 has a harder time finding time for activities, but once a month or so she makes a point of taking her kids to an event on campus. That way they feel at least a little bit connected to her life as a student.

MEALS AND EXERCISE

Going to college is stressful. In order to handle the stress, you need to be strong physically, mentally, and emotionally. You need to eat regularly and well, and you need to get some exercise. As the pressures of classwork and activities intensify, many students are tempted to skip their exercise; some begin skipping meals. Don't do it. Exercising regularly will give you more energy. And regular meals will give you the fuel you need to keep going. Besides, both meals and exercise are good excuses to take a break, to visit with your friends, to get away from schoolwork for a little while. Build meals and exercise into your weekly schedule.

LEISURE TIME

However you fill in the blank spaces in your schedule, leave some time for yourself. You can simply write in "relax," as the student in Figure 2.1 has done, or you can write in how you plan to use that time: play, visit with friends, watch TV, vegetate, whatever. And don't forget to write in time for the mundane details of life: doing your laundry, shopping, calling home.

Now that you have a preliminary schedule, put it in a place where you can refer to it often. Post it on your bulletin board, paste it inside the cover of your primary notebook, or tape it to the wall above your mirror. Follow it for a week. At the end of each day, take a final look at your schedule. Wherever you deviated from it, pencil in what you actually did during that hour. Be honest. No one is going to check your schedule to see how you spent your time.

At the end of the week look at the schedule you actually followed—the penciled-in parts. Now, reflect on whether or not what you actually did during the week contributed to your short-range goals. Did you keep up in your courses? Did you get the grades you need? Did you participate in the activities and go to the events and do all the things you needed to do to achieve your goals? If you did, the schedule you actually followed is a good one for you. Make a new version, incorporating the changes you made, and follow it for a week. Repeat this process, altering your schedule each week as needed to meet your goals.

If your week's activities did not contribute to your goals—if you fell behind in one or more courses, your grades were not as high as you need, or you missed some activities you wanted to participate in—then your schedule needs work. Chances are the schedule you designed was consistent with your goals; you just couldn't follow it. Why not? Were your goals unrealistic? Were you unwilling to spend the hours at study that you must spend to make top grades, or are you unable to spend the time in the weight room and at the training table that you must spend in order to make varsity? If that's the case, it's time to reexamine your goals. Perhaps law school is beyond your reach; perhaps making varsity is not worth the price you will have to pay.

Rewrite your schedule, striking a middle ground between the one you planned and the one you actually followed. If you planned to study 6 hours on Monday and you actually spent all of your time playing cards, try scheduling 3 hours for cards and 3 for study. If 3 hours of study on Mondays is good enough to reach your goals, your new schedule will work. If 3 hours of study will not get you the grades you need but it's the most you can do, then you may have to rewrite your goals.

Daily Schedules

Okay, now you have a weekly schedule; how do you follow it? You must refer to it often. Some students carry it with them, referring to it as they work through the day. Others post it on the wall over their desks. If you post your schedule in your room, use it to generate a daily schedule to carry around with you. Take a 3-by-5-inch card, jot the day's major events on it in sequence, and stick it in your pocket or purse. As you complete each task, check it off. Figures 2.4 and 2.5 depict the daily list of chores derived from the weekly schedule in Figures 2.1 and 2.2.

The single mother from Figure 2.3 got used to keeping her daily schedule in her datebook when she started selling houses years ago. Adding her class and study schedule to it was no chore at all.

Figure 2.4 *Daily chores: business major*

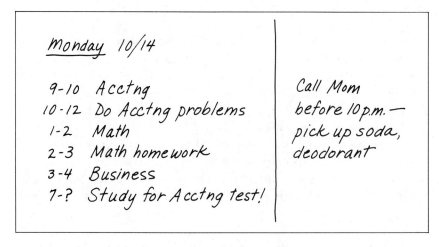

Monday 10/14

9-10	Acctng	Call Mom
10-12	Do Acctng problems	before 10 p.m. —
1-2	Math	pick up soda,
2-3	Math homework	deodorant
3-4	Business	
7-?	Study for Acctng test!	

Figure 2.5 *Daily chores: undecided major*

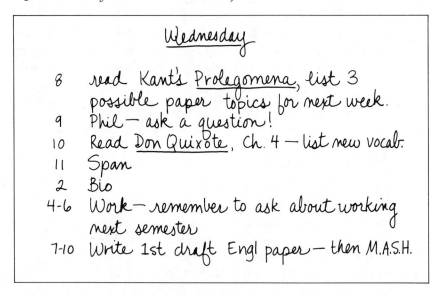

Wednesday

8   read Kant's Prolegomena, list 3
    possible paper topics for next week.
9   Phil — ask a question!
10 Read Don Quixote, Ch. 4 — list new vocab.
11 Span
2   Bio
4-6 Work — remember to ask about working
     next semester
7-10 Write 1st draft Engl paper — then M.A.S.H.

Wherever you keep your weekly schedule, make sure it's the first thing you look at in the morning and the last thing you look at before you go to bed. In the morning it will remind you what you had planned to do today. At night it will tell you what you have to look forward to tomorrow. And don't forget: Each night, write in what you actually did during each time block for the day.

Quarter/Semester Schedules

Some students like to plan out their entire quarter or semester in advance. If you expect to be under unusual time constraints from your work, family, and school responsibilities, a quarter or semester schedule is probably a good idea for you. Your college bookstore carries a selection of datebooks. Some devote a page per day, others devote a page (or facing pages) per week, others devote a page or two to a month. Take your pick; any one of them will do.

Use your datebook to plan your weekly schedule. (You may have to write very small.) As your instructors make assignments that are due in 2 weeks or a month, write them in. At the same time, write in when you plan to complete those assignments in the intervening weeks. Also, write in upcoming events you want to attend. When you plan each week's schedule, those assignments and events will already be in place.

Saying No

One of the hardest tasks for students, especially freshmen, is saying no. When the guy you admire from the floor above yours invites you to go downtown, it's hard to say no. When your best friend from home wants to talk on the phone for an hour and a half, it's hard to say no. When your pals try to talk you into playing volleyball on the beach, it's hard to say no.

But sometimes you must. If you have an exam coming and succeeding on that exam is important to you, you'd better say no. If you have scheduled 2 hours to work up your lab notes for tomorrow's chemistry class, you'd better say no. If you have to go to work in an hour and you planned to review your history notes first, you'd better say no.

Sometimes you can say yes, to be sure. If you can trade today's study time for tomorrow's leisure time without punishing yourself, do it. But make sure you complete the trade. When you are faced with temptation, look at your schedule. If the block of time in question has already been scheduled for play, no problem—go play. But if it has been scheduled for study, you should not give up that study time unless you can retrieve it later in the day, or tomorrow at the latest.

How can you say no without offending people you want to impress? One method is to stay out of temptation's way. Don't hang around the residence hall unless you are available for distraction. Do your studying elsewhere. Another way is to make your ambitions clear. "Gee, I'd really like to, but I've got this exam tomorrow and I need to do well. I want to go to law school." (Or stay eligible for football, or get into the business program, or whatever your ambition is.) College students generally respect ambitions; they wouldn't be in college if they didn't have some of their own.

A third method is to deflect the temptation. "I'd love to go. But can we do it tonight, after my exam?" Keep in mind that your new friends are probably trying to impress you as much as you are trying to impress them, so counterproposals are frequently well received. You might even be really bold, and suggest an alternative activity: "I've got this exam coming up in calculus, and I really need to study for it. But you're in calculus too; would you study with me?"

► EXERCISE 2.1 ◄

In your journal, reconstruct what happened the last time you failed to say no and regretted it later. Now rewrite the script. What would you have liked to say? What do you wish you had done? Finally, what can you do to avoid making the same mistake again?

The advantage of writing a schedule in advance is that it encourages you to make some of your decisions about how to spend your time rationally. Without a schedule you are likely to get carried away by the intoxication of all that free time. "Sure, I can go downtown; I don't have class until 4," you are likely to say, forgetting that you have a paper to write and an exam to study for. With a schedule posted on your wall, it's easier to remember your commitments.

The disadvantage of writing a schedule in advance is that it seems to take the spontaneity out of life. And spontaneity is one of the great charms of going to college. But you don't have to be a slave to your schedule. Even if you have scheduled 2 to 4 as study time, you can still go downtown—*as long as you make up the study time you lost.* The point of having a schedule is to make sure that you spend a certain number of hours studying, a certain number of hours in activities, a certain number of hours on yourself, and so on. Your schedule can be flexible, as long as the number of hours you have allocated for study, activities, and so on remains relatively constant.

EXERCISE 2.2

Write in your journal for 10 minutes about scheduling your time. List the advantages you see for yourself in writing a schedule in advance. List the disadvantages. Will the advantages outweigh the disadvantages? How?

Summary

Managing your time is a difficult task. You are faced with a world of new possibilities, and at the same time with the freedom to make your own choices. This chapter has shown you some ways to make your choices rationally, in a way that is consistent with your reasons for going to college in the first place.

1. Review your goals.
2. Schedule your fixed commitments.
3. Schedule your remaining time, in accordance with your long-, mid-, and short-range goals.
4. Each day, follow the schedule you have planned for yourself. Don't be a slave to it; your schedule should be flexible enough for you to make some changes on the fly. But if you give up study time, make sure that you make it up later.
5. At the end of each day, write what you actually did in each block of time on your schedule.
6. At the end of each week, review: Did your week's work contribute to your goals? Did you follow your schedule? Readjust your schedule as necessary for the following week.
7. Practice saying no, at least some of the time, when distractors come knocking on your door.

Attacking Your Coursework

➤ **Y**our goals are set, your preliminary schedule is posted on your wall; what next? How can you attack your courses so that you learn what you need to learn to achieve your goals?

College courses are different from the ones you took in high school. In high school, most of your teachers felt responsible for your learning. In college, most instructors believe that learning the material is your responsibility. They will give you the opportunity to learn through lectures, assignments, and answers to your questions during their office hours. Some will go further than that; many will not. The upshot is that you must take much more responsibility for your own learning than you did in high school.

This chapter will begin to show you how to do that. You will learn how to approach your first day of class, how to assess the sorts of work you will be required to do and how your own learning style fits those sorts of work, and how to get started in your classes.

The First Day of Class

The first meeting of a class is, in many ways, the most important meeting of that class during the quarter or semester. The typical instructor devotes at least a portion of the first meeting to distributing the syllabus or course outline, summarizing the broad objectives of the course, and telling you what she will expect of you. And from what she says, you can begin to figure out what you can expect from her.

Some students cut the first meeting of a class, thinking that nothing of substance goes on. They cheat themselves. It's true that many instructors don't begin covering the content of the course until the second meeting. (On the other hand, many instructors leap right in, knowing that students don't expect it.) But the information they give you on the first day is, in many respects, more important than the content of the course. So go to the first class, pay attention, take notes.

THE SYLLABUS

Almost every instructor will give you some sort of syllabus at the beginning of a course. It may be a single paragraph describing the sequence of topics to be covered; it may be a list of assignments, categorized by week or day; it may be a complete outline describing what will happen in each class meeting. It may include a paragraph or two describing the instructor's goals for the course. It may include the policies and procedures the instructor intends to follow. It may include the instructor's formula for computing your final grade. All of that information is valuable to you.

Figure 3.1 shows what a typical syllabus looks like.

Reading the syllabus tells you a great deal about what you will have to do to succeed in Speech Communication 101. First of all, the instructor likes to be called Doctor Bryan; otherwise he wouldn't list his name that way. Second, there will be a lot of reading. Fortunately the reading assignments are divided up by week, so you should be able to keep up. Third, the weekly quizzes mean that you can never, ever miss class on Friday; losing even a few of the 80 points for quizzes would kill your final grade. Fourth, the midterm and final exams are worth a total of 250 points. If you study hard for them you should be able to earn 200 points at least. If you earn 7s on the quizzes and 50 points on the paper, you'll end up with 304 points—a low B. If a C is acceptable, scale your plans down; if you are shooting for an A, scale up.

Now look at the list of topics. It gives you a capsule summary of the course. First, note that Speech Communication 101 is not going to teach you to speak better; it will teach you about communication through speaking. Second, there are many ways humans communicate through speaking. We communicate verbally and nonverbally;

Figure 3.1 *Sample syllabus* (Adapted from Charles Braithwaite, New Mexico State University)

```
                    Speech Communication 101
      Dr. William Jennings Bryan, Johnson Hall 212, ext. 634

Office hours: Mon 9-10, M-Th 1-2, and by appointment

Texts:    (1) C. Book (editor), Human Communication:
          Principles, Contexts, and Skills, N.Y., St.
          Martin's Press, 1980.

          (2) J. Civikly (editor), Contexts of
          Communication, N.Y., Holt, Rinehart & Winston,
          1981.

Quizzes and Exams: On Friday of each week I will give a
20-minute quiz, primarily on the reading material for
the week. I will give one midterm exam following Unit IV
and a comprehensive final. Quizzes cannot be made up;
exams can be made up only if you bring me an official
excuse signed by the dean.

Paper: You will write a five-page paper on a topic of
your choice. (However, I must approve your topic.)
The paper is due 1 week before the final. No late papers
will be accepted, under any circumstances.

Grading: Each of the nine quizzes will count 10 points.
I will throw out your lowest quiz score when computing
your grade. The midterm counts 100 points, the final
150, the paper 70. Thus you can earn a maximum of
400 points. 350-400 = A; 300-349 = B; 250-299 = C;
200-249 = D; below 200 = F.

Topics to be discussed, roughly by week:

I.    Historical overview of speech communication.
      Reading: (1), Chapter 3.

II.   Theoretical perspectives in human communication.
      Reading: (1), Chapter 1; (2) Chapters 1, 2, 3.

III.  Verbal and nonverbal communication.
      Reading: (1), Chapter 2; (2) Chapters 11, 12.

IV.   Interpersonal/relational communication.
      Reading: (1), Chapter 4; (2) Chapters 9, 10, 5,
      6, 8.

                                        (continued)
```

```
    V.     Family communication.
           Reading: (2), Chapter 4.

    VI.    Small group communication.
           Reading: (1), Chapter 5; (2), Chapters 12, 14, 15.

    VII.   Organizational communication.
           Reading: (1) Chapters 6, 8; (2) Chapters 16, 17,
           18, 30.

    VIII.  Mass communication.
           Reading: (1) Chapter 7; (2) Chapters 22, 23,
           24, 31.

    IX.    Cultural/intercultural communication.
           Reading: (2) Chapters 25, 26, 27.


    If you are having difficulty understanding the material,
    please come and see me in my office.
```

we communicate in families, small groups, and organizations; we communicate to the masses. Third, each of those ways is different in some respects from each of the other ways—you know that because each type of communication is listed as a separate topic. This list of topics tells you the major categories of material you will be studying. Knowing what they are in advance will help you organize the material as you study it.

Now you can begin planning how you will attack this course. The reading load is fairly heavy, and there are regular quizzes and exams; it looks as if studying for this course will consume at least 2 hours for every hour you spend in class. And toward the end of the quarter there is a substantial writing assignment; that means more time when you can least afford it. Perhaps you could start that paper a few weeks earlier.

Try to figure out which of the assignments will be the most helpful in learning the material and which will count the most toward your grade. They may not be the same. And that may be important to you. If you are taking the course as a foundation for majoring in speech communication, you must learn the basic principles. But if you are taking the course to fill out your general education requirement, then just earning an acceptable grade may be your goal.

Finally, begin scheduling the work. Guess how much time it will take to complete the first week's assignment, and write it in your calendar. If you are keeping a calendar for the quarter or semester, write in at least the major assignments.

Pay close attention to the passing remarks on policies and procedures for the class: "Quizzes cannot be made up; exams can be made up only if you bring me an official excuse signed by the dean." "No late papers will be accepted, under any circumstances." Many instructors will tell you their policies in the syllabus and thereafter assume that you know them. If you violate a policy unknowingly later in the quarter, they are frequently unsympathetic. "I'm sorry that your grandmother died, but I don't give make-up tests except for officially excused absences; didn't you read the syllabus?"

Some syllabi go into far greater depth than this one. They might include statements of the course objectives, brief summaries of the lectures, reviews of the texts, questions for weekly review, sample exams, and the names of the instructor's dog and cat. These syllabi make wonderful study guides. Make a habit of looking over the review questions and sample exams before you do your reading. Those questions tell you what the instructor thinks is important in each chapter. And when you visit her in her office, make a point of asking how Flopsy and Mopsy are.

On the other hand, some syllabi are very sketchy. You may receive a mimeographed scrap of paper telling you the instructor's office hours, the name of the text, and a very tentative schedule: "Probably a midterm, certainly a final, and I think I'll have you write a paper or two." But even that much information is helpful. It tells you that you are not likely to get any feedback from this instructor on how you are doing in the course for a very long time. If getting a good grade in this course is important to you, it would be wise to begin speaking with the instructor early in the quarter or semester. Tell him your concerns, and ask if there is some way he can assess your chances of doing well.

Hang on to your syllabus. Store it away in your notebook, your course folder, or your desk drawer. Refer to it occasionally to see what's coming up, to remind yourself of major assignments, to refresh your knowledge of policies and procedures, and to predict your course grade.

```
┌─────────────────────────────────────────────────────────────────┐
│               ███████ EXERCISE 3.1 ◄───────────────             │
│                                                                   │
│   **Examine the syllabus** for one of the courses you are taking. In │
│   your journal, answer these questions. (1) What grade do you     │
│   need in this course to achieve your goals? (2) How can you earn │
│   that grade? (3) Will you have to study more or less than 2 hours │
│   for every hour spent in class?                                  │
│        Repeat this exercise for each of your courses.             │
│                                                                   │
└─────────────────────────────────────────────────────────────────┘
```

Unfortunately there are still instructors who refuse to give their students a syllabus. What can you do when that happens? On the first day of class, ask some pointed questions. "How will you compute our grades?" "How many exams will there be?" "What are your office hours?" "Will you be using any additional texts later in the semester?" Don't be rude, but don't be put off either. You are paying for this course; you have a right to know how it will be structured.

Learning Styles

One of the things you can learn from the first day in class is what sort of work a course will require. Speech Communication 101 requires lots of reading, regular review for quizzes and exams, and a little writing. Your mathematics course may require no reading but lots of problem sets. Your biology course may require lots of laboratory work—performing experiments, preparing lab reports, and thinking about the implications of your experiments.

Each of these different sorts of work demands a different sort of learning. To learn from reading, you must grasp the author's concepts and make them your own. To learn from working problems, you must figure out how to solve each problem and then combine those methods into a general principle. To learn from laboratories, you must grasp a conceptual framework and understand how the specific events in the lab fit into and verify it.

All people do not learn in all of these ways equally well. There are tests you can take to find out precisely what your learning style is. Your college's counseling center can administer them and interpret the results for you. Check it out; you'll learn a lot about yourself.

But even without taking a test, you can analyze your own learning style. Do you like to get the big picture, to understand the broad concepts? If so, you are a "lumper." You probably learn well from books and lectures, especially where the writer or speaker deals in generalizations; Speech Communication 101 is made to order for you. In your math and laboratory courses you probably like to understand the general principles before you leap into problem sets or labs. And the specific techniques to be used may be difficult for you to master.

Do you prefer to learn by amassing detail? Then you are a "splitter." The details of speech communication will come easily to you, as will the specific techniques in your math and lab courses. The general concepts of those courses may be harder for you to remember.

If you are a lumper, you should feel at home in the traditional liberal arts courses in college. Lumpers do well with broad concepts, because they like to begin by understanding the big picture; most liberal arts courses deal in broad concepts. Lumpers work best on their own, by internalizing those general concepts and fitting them into their previous experience; most liberal arts courses expect you to work on your own. In fact, most liberal arts faculty are lumpers, and they tend to design their assignments for people like them.

Lumpers sometimes run into trouble by concentrating so much on generalizations that they have no grasp of the particulars at all. When they have to apply a generalization they may run into serious trouble—for instance, when they have to solve a problem in calculus or physics, or when they have to give specific instances of a general concept. If you are a lumper, you should practice applying the generalizations you learn. For every concept you learn, learn a specific application of it as well. For every theory, learn a particular case where the theory applies. For every general principle, learn some examples that demonstrate its truth.

Splitters never have that problem. They have enough detail at their fingertips to solve any problem, to apply any theory. Splitters tend to prefer hands-on courses, such as accounting, math, or the sciences, where command of detail counts. Splitters always have enough detail, but they may have trouble understanding and using the broad concepts. If you are a splitter, you must make sure that you understand not only the detail, but the framework within which that detail fits. For instance, in calculus you must know all of the formulas that the instructor might ask you to use on the test—that's the detail. But you should also know the theoretical framework that ties those formulas together. For only through knowing that framework will you know which formula to use to solve a particular problem.

In history, you must know the major events, their dates, and the names of the major players—these make up the detail. But you must also understand the historical setting, the motivations of the major figures, and the causal sequence of those events—the framework. Without knowing the framework, you cannot write good answers to essay questions, and you may have difficulty with imaginatively written multiple-choice questions as well.

How can splitters make sure they understand the framework? The first step is to understand that you are a splitter and that detail is easy for you to learn but concepts are harder. That knowledge will help you concentrate on concepts as you listen to lectures, read your texts, and study for exams. Write down theory as well as fact. Try to place each fact you learn in the context of a theory, or at least in the context of a collection of facts. Second, work with others to make sure that you do, in fact, understand the appropriate concepts. Ask the instructor, study with friends, or read someone else's notes. What if you are a lumper determined to go into engineering, a field that demands mastery of enormous amounts of detail? All is not lost. Take advantage of your ability to generalize, to understand the broad concepts, and to grasp the basic categories by filling in those generalizations and concepts and categories with a wealth of detail. Understanding that you are a lumper, that you have a tendency to gloss over detail, will help you concentrate on specifics as you study. Whenever you learn a new theory, make sure that you can apply it. Write out some applications: solutions to real problems, or extensions of the theory to a new realm, or a specific implication of the theory. When the exam comes, you should be ready both to reproduce the theory and to apply it.

Actually, all of us are both lumpers and splitters. We can all grasp general concepts, and we can all master detail. But each one of us tends to prefer either learning concepts first (lumpers) or detail first (splitters). The key is to understand your own tendency to learn in one way, and then concentrate on learning in the other way as well.

Whenever you are gathering facts, work on organizing them into a theoretical framework. Whenever you are learning a theory, work on learning the facts that the theory explains. You can do that easily while you read, because you control the pace. It's not quite so easy when you listen to a lecture, but practice helps. And when you review your notes you can easily write in extra facts to support a theory—or theory to tie together facts.

Lumpers prefer to process information in one way; splitters in another. We also have preferences in how we obtain our information.

Some of us gather information best by reading. Readers frequently get good grades in school, because most schoolwork involves lots of reading. Others learn best by actually seeing something; once you have a visual framework, you can hang all sorts of information on it. Pictures help, but direct visual experience is the best. Others learn best through conversations with others, where you can listen for a while, then ask questions to get some additional information, and finally add some experiences of your own to fill in the gaps.

Some of us learn best by actually messing about with things: "Oh, I see, this goes here, and *that's* why it works that way." Lab courses fit this learning style well. So do field experiences: internships, student teaching, field trips attached to science courses, and so on. Unfortunately, few freshmen have access to field experiences.

Just as we are all both lumpers and splitters, all of us can learn in lots of ways, but we all prefer one or two ways over the others. You should be aware of the ways you prefer. Your learning style should help determine how you attack your coursework. If you need a visual framework, for instance, movies, old newspapers and magazines, and books of photographs will be essential study aids for your twentieth-century history course. If you learn well through conversations, study groups will help you enormously.

How do you react to time pressure? Some students can only work if they are under the gun—a paper due tomorrow or an exam in 2 hours. Unfortunately, there frequently isn't enough time to complete the task if you wait for the pressure to build. Sometimes you can create the necessary pressure for yourself by creating artificial deadlines. "Let's see, this paper's due Friday, but if I wait until Thursday night to start like I did last time I'll probably get another C−. But if I can do an outline by Wednesday, I'll be ahead—okay, by Wednesday supper I'll have an outline for my paper!"

Other students wilt under pressure and need to start well in advance of the deadline. If that's you, pay close attention to the syllabus so that you know all of the deadlines long before they are upon you. And if one of your instructors sometimes gives pop quizzes, always be prepared.*

---

*A small percentage of our college students (estimates range from a handful to 10 percent) suffer from learning disabilities. Students with learning disabilities may reverse letters while reading or be unable to write the sentences they can speak. Students with very mild disabilities have usually learned to compensate for them by the time they get to college. But students with serious learning disabilities—acute dyslexia, for example—will have a very difficult time in college. Fortunately, most colleges have recognized that students with learning disabilities are not stupid and that they can

Write for 20 minutes in your journal about your own learning style. First, answer these questions.

1. When you are learning something new, do you try to grasp the basic concept first or do you prefer to gather lots of detail—that is, are you a lumper or a splitter?
2. Do you learn best by reading about something, by seeing it, by talking about it, or by actually working with it?
3. Do you prefer to study by yourself or with others?
4. Do you work well under the pressure of deadlines or do you prefer to get a head start?

Now for each of your courses, analyze the type of work being assigned. Will it be presented in broad concepts or will you be given a lot of details and expected to form the broad concepts yourself? Will it require learning from someone else's words, either through reading or lecture? Or will it require learning through your own direct experience, through a laboratory or working problems or practicing? Write your answers in your journal.

Finally, write about how your own learning style fits each of your courses. Do you foresee any problems? What will you do about them?

Attacking Coursework Through Using Language

Remember when you were in third grade and had to memorize a poem? Remember how you did it, either by saying it over and over or by writing it over and over? You have probably used that technique

---

learn as much as anyone else, with a little assistance. Most will provide special advising, tutoring, taping of textbooks, or whatever compensatory services are necessary. If reading and writing seem unusually difficult for you, it is possible that you suffer from a learning disability. Go to your counseling or testing center and tell them of your suspicions. They will give you a battery of tests to find out; if you are learning disabled, they will provide a course of action for you.

to learn all kinds of things ever since. Sometimes you used it intentionally. You may have learned a part for a play or a piece of music by rehearsing it over and over (first by yourself, later with the rest of the cast or group) or memorized chemistry formulas by writing them 100 times in your notebook. Other times you used that technique without realizing it. You probably can recite the starting lineup of your favorite team or sing the verses of your children's favorite bedtime songs simply because you've repeated them so much.

I won't suggest that you use repetition as your basic learning technique in college. There simply isn't enough time in the day to repeat everything you must learn. (You will find, however, that repetition is an excellent way to learn lists of words or dates, formulas, or rules of conjugation—all those things that are hard to learn any other way.) And the crucial part of this technique is not the repeating; it's the using of language.

There is a direct connection between your memory and your writing hand. When you write something down, you tend to remember it. When you write it down two or three times, you will remember it longer. Same with your tongue; it's directly connected to your memory, so that when you say something it tends to stick in your mind. Just using language, either in writing or speech, helps you remember.

WRITING

No doubt you take notes in at least some of your classes. Most students think the only reason for taking notes is to have something to study when preparing for the test. Not so. The most important reason for taking notes is to help you engage your brain. When you take notes you pay attention, you concentrate on the subject matter, and you think about what's going on in class. As a result, you tend to remember what your instructor was saying.

When you stop taking notes, your mind wanders. You think about what you have to do for tomorrow's biology lab or tonight's party or the weekend's trip home. You don't think about what's going on in class. And you don't remember afterward what the instructor was saying.

Some students try to make up for classes they missed by copying someone else's notes. It doesn't work very well. For one thing, each of us takes notes in a highly individualized way; one person's well-organized, clearly written notes are another person's gobbledygook. But the major reason borrowed notes won't help is that the borrower wasn't in class when the notes were taken. Taking notes—writing while you are listening—helps fix the contents of a lecture in your head. When you review your notes, you remember what you heard. But if you missed the lecture, you have nothing to remember. Consequently the notes are not very helpful. (If you must miss a class, ask a friend or the instructor for a brief summary of the lecture. *Then* borrow notes. And never think that you can skip a lecture and adequately catch up by borrowing notes.)

Taking notes is a valuable exercise even if you never look at your notes again. When you take notes you are using words, using language. And using language helps keep you actively engaged in your schoolwork. Of course, taking notes is even more valuable when you *do* look at them again. Chapter 7 will teach you some techniques for taking and using notes effectively.

But what about outside of class? Going to college is a lot more than taking notes from lectures. You learn through your studying: reading, working problems, and studying for examinations. You learn through laboratory courses, through field trips, through conferences with your instructors during office hours, through bull sessions with your roommate or spouse or children, and through simply thinking about everything you are experiencing. Is there a way to take notes on those experiences too, so that you can pay maximum attention to them and remember what you learned?

Certainly. Whenever you study, you should be writing. If you are reading, take notes; if you are working problems, take notes on the methods you are learning; if you are preparing for an examination, write some potential questions and their answers. *Never* study without a pencil in your hand. It's the same as being in class: If you're not taking notes, chances are you're not paying attention.

Take a walk through the library or the study lounge of your residence hall. Among the students you see studying, who is more actively engaged: those writing things down or those who are just reading? Take a closer look at the students who are just reading. They are passive: Their eyes are glazed, they fiddle with their books, they slump backwards, they look around a lot. Now take a look at the ones who are writing. They are actively participating in their study: They sit forward, they are not easily distracted, they are concentrating. Using a pencil is an enormous aid to effective studying. (Chapter 8 will show you some techniques for taking notes while you study.)

Writing is built into most laboratory courses, in the form of lab books or field books. In your lab book you are taught to record everything you do that might have an effect on your experiment, so you have a record to trace what might have affected the result. In your field book you record your various observations in the field for later analysis. But successful science students use their lab and field books for much more than that. They record useful procedures, they note unexpected observations, they speculate on the meaning of the experiments they are performing, they wonder about the origins of what they see. They use their lab books to help their thinking.

But what about when you're not studying or in lab or on a field trip; what about when you're talking to your instructor or your roommate or simply thinking about things? How can writing help you then? The simplest way is to keep a journal, much like the journal you are using for the exercises in this book.

A journal is a private notebook in which you record anything you feel like recording. You can use it to remember things for later use. Summarize a meeting with your composition instructor so that you can remember what he said when you write your next paper, or jot down the idea for a math project that came to you during breakfast, or list the seven events that led to the Civil War in anticipation of a snap quiz in history.

You can use your journal to think on paper. Scribble a rough outline for your next essay in political science, or sketch out a program for computer science, or draft a letter to the dean petitioning for an exception to the minimum class load requirement. You can use it to plan for the future: schedule your study time for the afternoon, or your major assignments for the quarter, or your short- and mid-range goals for each course. And you can use it for personal tasks: reminiscing about high school successes to make you feel better on a bad day, working out your family budget for the month, figuring out what to do about the lonesome boyfriend back home.

A loose-leaf binder works best for a journal—it allows you to add paper, reorganize your entries, and take out and reinsert ideas for essays—but any sort of notebook will do. Some students use one large loose-leaf binder for everything: lecture and reading notes, journal, letters home, grocery list. That's okay, as long as you keep those different functions separate with tabbed dividers. Other students use separate spiral-bound notebooks for lecture and reading notes for each of their courses and a small loose-leaf for their journals. Whatever works for you is wonderful.

Some students keep a study log in their journals. Whenever they finish studying a particular subject, they write in their journals for 5 or 10 minutes, summarizing and reacting to what they studied. Suppose you've just spent 2 hours working calculus problems. When you finish, do a brief journal-write on the techniques you were applying. Or after reading philosophy for an hour, write for 5 minutes on the most important single point the author made. Just as with class notes, the important thing is not what you write or what you do with your journal entries (though you may find them useful some time in the future)—it's that you are writing. When you are writing you are also thinking. What you think about, you tend to remember.

EXERCISE 3.3

In your journal, write for 5 minutes on the most interesting lesson you have learned so far in this chapter. Wait! Don't look back at what you've just read. You should do this exercise off the top of your head, without reviewing. Be sure to write for 5 minutes without stopping. And let your mind work. Explore on paper the implications of that lesson for your life.

When you have completed this journal-write, reflect for a moment on what you did. Was it helpful? Did writing about what you had just read help you learn? Did the writing lead to some thinking about your own life as a student? Would writing in your journal after every reading assignment be a worthwhile use of your time?

Of course you'll be doing a fair amount of writing in your classes above and beyond your notes and your journal. The writing you do for your classes—short essays, term papers, lab reports, essay exams, and so on—will help keep you actively engaged in your schoolwork. Take that sort of writing seriously. The major principle of this section is that writing will help you learn. It follows that the more you write, the more you will learn. We have seen that notes and journals help you learn by helping you think. That's true of the writing you do for class as well.

Too many students think of writing for class as simply earning a grade. It does that, true, but it also does a great deal more. Short essays and essay questions give you the opportunity to organize some bits of knowledge around a central theme. Term papers let you gather large amounts of knowledge into one document. Lab reports encourage you to think about your experiment and draw some conclusions. In each case, you are gathering information, processing it in your mind, and transmitting it to the written page. The act of transmission—the writing—will help some of it stick. In short, when you write about something, you know it. You can make use of that knowledge on the final examination, in your later courses, and maybe even after you graduate.

In one respect, writing for class is very different from note taking and journal writing. Your essays, reports, and exams are written for someone else—your instructor. She will grade them. Your notes and your journal are written to yourself; no one will grade them. That's an important difference. In your journal you can afford to write anything you feel like, no matter how foolish; no one will grade you down. In your notes you can use whatever spelling and punctuation make sense to you; no one will crab at you about mechanics.

Still, any kind of writing is a valuable aid to the learning process, whether your audience is yourself or your instructor. Or your mom. Your letters home can be a valuable tool for thinking about your experiences at college, for reflecting on the changes you are going through. The value is in the process of writing, of putting meaningful sequences of words down on a sheet of paper. Some of the meaning stays with you.

SPEAKING

Most of us speak more than we write. We speak in a wide variety of situations: at the breakfast table (grunts), during class (cryptic remarks to the guy in the next seat), in conferences with your instructor (reasonably well-formed sentences), and so on. Sometimes our speech is important, and sometimes it does little more than pass the time. But notice that whenever we use spoken language, we are investing sounds with meaning. In a similar fashion, whenever we write, we are investing squiggles on a page with meaning. Whenever you invest something with meaning, be it a sound or a squiggle, you are thinking. Thinking is the first step to learning. Therefore speaking can help you learn, just as writing can help you learn.

A character in a George Bernard Shaw play gets a big laugh by saying, "How can I know what I think until I hear what I say?" There's a lot of truth in that remark. We frequently don't know what we think about a particular topic until we talk about it. As we talk we spin out our opinions, we bring in new supporting evidence, we consider and dispose of opposing viewpoints, we reach our conclusions. Try this experiment: Pay attention to the next discussion you hear in the residence hall or at home. See if the participants change their opinions while they speak. If they do, they have been demonstrating the truth of Shaw's line.

We think as we speak, just as we think as we write. How can you take advantage of that phenomenon to help you learn? Well, you already know some of the ways: repeating a poem over and over until you know it, practicing your lines for a play, rehearsing a speech. Take advantage of them. When you must memorize something, repeat it aloud over and over; you'll soon know it. When you have to perform orally, in a play or in speech class or anywhere else, practice your performance in front of another person. Don't worry about looking silly—everybody looks silly sometimes. And looking silly is a small price to pay for learning what you need to learn.

There are some additional ways of using speaking to help you learn; you might not be aware of these methods. First, use your conversations. Conversing is one of the most basic human functions; all of us do it. And all of us learn a great deal through our conversations, both through the information we take in by listening to others and through what we hear ourselves say. Most of what you know about popular culture—music, movies, TV, fiction, sports—you learned through conversations with your peers. And you learned it painlessly. Well, you can learn a great deal about your classes just as painlessly by turning some of your conversations to your schoolwork.

Make a point of asking the guy next to you in economics class about that weird graph on page 73. He may not understand it either, but the two of you together can probably make sense of it. Or ask the folks you have lunch with about the convocation speaker: Did anybody understand what she was talking about? Someone will have a notion of what she meant, and that will spark an idea in you, and someone else will have a relevant story to tell, and before you know it you will have gathered a much more complete understanding. And that understanding will stick with you because you were an active participant in the conversation.

You can use this technique in any number of ways. Chat regularly with your roommate about the lectures in the history course you both take; summarize for your spouse what you learned in school over dinner each evening; talk with your teammates about how to balance athletics and schoolwork; discuss yesterday's lecture with the guy next to you just before class starts. You'll learn a lot, much of what you learn will be valuable, and most of it will stick with you.

Second, take every opportunity you can to speak. Volunteer to make oral presentations, ask and answer questions in class, and visit your instructors during their office hours. The more practice you get using spoken language, the easier it becomes. The easier it is for you to speak, the more you use language with facility. And the more facile you are with words, the more thinking you do while you are using them and the more you learn.

EXERCISE 3.4

Resolve to ask at least one question in each of your classes this week. Can't think of any? List three questions for each class in your journal before class starts. And during class jot questions in the margin of your notes.

Using language, either through writing or speaking, is a wonderful way to attack your coursework. When you are writing or speaking about what you are studying, you are automatically thinking about it. And when you think, you will learn and remember.

Summary

On the first day of class you can begin to see how each of your courses can help you meet your goals. The syllabus will tell you what is expected of you. Through your own knowledge of your learning style, you can figure out some of your learning strategies. And through writing and speaking about your coursework, you can begin to absorb the details and principles you must master in order to succeed.

CHAPTER 4

Learning Outside of Class

Student life is strange. If you live in a residential college, you exist in a protected environment, but within that environment you enjoy a wide and rich set of choices. You are treated like a child in that you are still in school preparing for adult life. Yet you are treated like an adult as well; you are expected to make responsible choices and you are held responsible for their consequences.

If you are an adult who has returned to school, student life is stranger yet. Outside of school you have an adult's responsibilities: a job, perhaps a family to support, a home of your own to maintain, car payments, and so on. But in school you are treated, in many ways, like a schoolchild.

Previous chapters have helped you develop some goals for your college career, a schedule to help you meet those goals, and some strategies for attacking your coursework. This chapter will show you that your life outside of class can be, should be, as valuable to you and to your education as the time you spend in class.

To the traditional 18-year-old freshman, college looks like a bunch of courses to take—that's work—and a list of activities—that's fun. One of the aims of this book is to convince you that the work you do for your courses can be at least satisfying, and sometimes fun. The purpose of this chapter is to convince you that you can learn from your entertaining activities. The net effect is that the line between work and fun blurs.

To the adult starting college after being out of school for a while, it all looks like a bunch of requirements to be fulfilled in order to get what you want—a degree, a certification, a license, or whatever. Many returning adults think that their lives outside of class are completely divorced from their classwork. This chapter will show you that your work, your family life, and your recreational activities can enrich your classwork.

Getting Involved

Look at the students you know. Chances are that the busiest students are the ones who are the most successful, and that the students who are always watching TV or lounging around the residence hall are the ones who are least successful. And the busiest students are busy with activities outside of class as well as with their coursework. The point is that students who are actively engaged in what they are doing, both inside and outside the classroom, succeed in college.

In order for you to succeed, you should become actively engaged in some activities outside of the classroom as well. What you become involved in matters little; the important thing is becoming involved. An on- or off-campus job will do it, or maintaining a family, or engaging in an undergraduate research project, or athletics, or politics (campus or off-campus), or a food cooperative, or a volunteer activity of some sort—the list of available activities is endless.

Whatever your outside-of-class activity is, you must be responsible to it. Being responsible to your outside-of-class activity will help you be responsible to your coursework. Having a lot to do will stimulate you to schedule your time efficiently. And being responsible to your activity as well as your coursework will give you something else to think about besides school.

Some of your outside-of-class activities will contribute directly to your coursework, thereby helping you reach your academic goals. Field trips can give you visual images to match the words in your texts. Informal contacts with professors can help you learn the language and the culture of their academic disciplines, and that will help you grasp the framework for the courses they teach. Lectures, concerts, art shows, athletic events, receptions, performances, and the rest of the extracurricular activities your college offers you can enrich and supplement what you learn in class. Internships, directed and independent study, research opportunities, and cooperative education arrangements can fill out the generalizations of your coursework with specific applications. They can also forge a link between your schooling and your career.

Other activities will contribute less directly to your coursework. A job, for instance, will pay some of your bills, thereby allowing you to be a student. Your social life will keep you connected to the people who support you the most. Your exercise will keep you healthy and alert. But each one of these activities will also give you learning opportunities that will supplement what you are learning in the classroom.

Cocurricular Activities

Many of the courses you take will build in some extra activities as supplementary learning activities. Academics call them cocurricular activities. Some students ignore them, thinking that the real learning is what goes on in the classroom. They are wrong. Cocurricular activities enrich your classroom learning.

FIELD TRIPS

Some professors love field trips. Your geology class may go on a trip to look at significant outcrops of rock; cultural anthropology may include a visit to a nearby archaeological dig; social psychology may build in a tour of a mental hospital.

Take advantage of as many of these trips as possible. Most of them will help you immensely in the class for which they are arranged. Actually seeing the variegated strata of sedimentary rock is infinitely better than relying on the pictures and charts in your geology text—especially if you are a visual learner. Hearing a practicing archaeologist talk about the mundane details of anthropology in the field will bring your boring readings to life. Witnessing what actually goes on in a mental hospital will allow you to add significant detail to the essays you write for your psychology class.

These trips will help you in your other classes as well. The details you witnessed in the mental hospital can add spice to your paper for film criticism on *The Lost Weekend*. Your trip to the archaeological dig can be the subject of a presentation for speech communication. The behavior of your fellow students when the geology bus broke down can be the basis for a sociology research project. And so on. There is no substitute for experience; field trips give you first-hand experiences that will put living flesh on the dry bones you are studying in class.

SOCIAL EVENTS

If one of your professors invites you to an informal event, such as a reception for a visiting scholar or a departmental beer party, don't think twice about it. Dress nicely, put on your company manners and practice your winning smile, and go. You'll see your instructors as real people, not just as talking heads. They have families who argue, cars that don't run, and pets that are out of control, just as you do. Seeing them as real people will help you take them seriously in class. By the same token, seeing you as a real person—not just as a name in a grade book—will help your professors take you seriously in class.

Informal events like these can also help you understand the academic environment. You might see a pair of English professors arguing vehemently about modes of literary criticism, or a covey of mathematicians discussing the four-color map problem. You'll learn that academics take their work very seriously and that they are almost always thinking about it. Knowing that will help you understand why your English instructor was so offended when you dismissed Emily Dickinson as a mewling adolescent or why your mathematics professor graded you down for reversing a sign. You may be entranced by the academic culture, in which case you should think seriously about graduate school. You may be appalled by it. In either case, understanding it will help you succeed in class.

REVIEW SESSIONS

Some instructors will schedule optional review sessions before major exams. If doing well in the course is important to your goals, go. Bring whatever questions you have and ask them. Listen to the questions others ask and to the answers. Pay particular attention to any remarks the instructor makes about the upcoming exam. These sessions will not only give you a chance to ask any questions that trouble you, they will give you an insight into what questions are likely to appear on the test and how they should be answered.

SPECIAL PROGRAMS

Colleges frequently design special academic programs for special purposes. Honors programs, for instance, give ambitious students the chance to learn faster or learn more than their less ambitious peers. Developmental or remedial programs help underprepared students catch up. If you fit into one of these categories, leap into the program that fits you. It will give you some academic opportunities that are probably not available to you elsewhere, it will teach you some things you need to know earlier than you could otherwise learn them, and it will give you a more intimate home within the college community.

Even if there's not a special program for you, you can still get involved in activities that are directly related to your field of study. If you are a theater major, volunteer to work behind the scenes. If you are in music, go out for the band or orchestra. If you want to be a teacher, volunteer for the campus tutoring program. If you hope to be a coach, go out for a sport and offer to coach Little League in your hometown.

LEARNING CENTERS

Most colleges have learning centers that offer tutoring services, help in math, developmental classes for students who are underprepared, assistance for writing projects, advising, study skills training, and so on. They are called a variety of names, including Learning Center, Academic Assistance Center, Skills Center, Writing Room, Math Place, Developmental Programs, HELP Center, and so on. You probably heard about at least one during freshman orientation.

Many schools have a learning center designed specifically for returning adults (or "nontraditional students," as they are frequently called in higher education). The folks there will advise you on appropriate courses, on how to take advantage of your out-of-school experiences, on how to brush up on your reading and note-taking and study skills, on how to remember all of the math you have forgotten. For students who have been out of school for more than a year or two, using these centers is crucial.

Some colleges require certain students to use the learning center. If you were admitted on a probationary basis, for instance, the dean may tell you that using the Academic Skills Center's services is mandatory until you prove yourself in the classroom. Or if your math placement test score was low, your adviser may tell you to take a developmental math course at the HELP Center before you tackle

College Algebra. Other schools will strongly encourage some students—prized athletes or students with disabilities—to use the learning center. On the other hand, using the learning center may be entirely voluntary.

In any case, you should use it, even if you are a solid student earning good grades in all of your classes. The learning center can help you become a better student, no matter where you are starting from. If you are struggling in basic math, they can help you pass; if you need a B in anthropology, they can help you earn it; if you need straight As to get into veterinary school, they can advise you on how to do it.

The staff in the learning center is responsible for helping you succeed. They have some good resources to put at your disposal, including (in many schools) student tutors who have succeeded in the courses you are struggling with. Furthermore, participating in a workshop on study skills, or taking a basic math class, or getting help in an English paper at the learning center will help you get involved in your coursework.

INTERNSHIPS

Most colleges offer internship or cooperative education programs. All colleges that certify teachers offer practice teaching opportunities for education majors. These programs give students the opportunity to study on campus for 2 or 3 years and then to put what they have learned to work in a real job setting. The advantages are enormous. These programs allow you to check out your interest in and fitness for a particular line of work before you commit yourself. At the same time they give you the opportunity to impress a potential employer. And they give you a break from classes, just when you want one the most. Some of them will even pay you for your time.

Unfortunately, internships, co-op education, and practice teaching are seldom available to freshmen, or even to sophomores. But you can plan ahead. Discuss the possibilities of an internship with your adviser, and build one into your long-range plan if it seems appropriate. Chapter 9 will give you more details about internships, which will assist your planning. In the meantime, find other ways to build relevant work experience into your academic program.

UNDERGRADUATE RESEARCH

Many colleges offer undergraduates the chance to engage in research, usually in conjunction with a faculty member. In some places these opportunities come through a program of grants directly to the student; in others, professors have budgets to hire students to work with them. Many of these programs are weighted toward the sciences and social sciences, but not all. Research, in this context, means scholarly activity. Humanists do research also, and some of the research they do requires student assistants. If your school offers these opportunities, take advantage. Doing a research project on your own, helping a professor with her research, or even typing manuscripts will help you learn in much the same way an internship will help you learn. And sometimes you'll get paid.

STUDY ABROAD

All schools encourage their students to travel. Some offer junior year abroad programs, some promote summer study on other campuses, some simply offer information about opportunities to study elsewhere. Try to take advantage of at least one of those opportunities to study through travel during your undergraduate years. These programs are usually expensive; you may have to scrimp and save and borrow to do it. That's okay; you will remember your experiences long after you have forgotten the hardships you endured to pay for them.

Some colleges follow the 4-1-4 schedule: 4 months of class, 1 month of intersession (some schools call it J-term, for January term), 4 months of class. The intersession is meant for independent study, extended field trips, intense seminars, and other educational experiences that don't fit very well into semesters. Many freshmen tend to think of the intersession as an extra vacation. Don't use it that way. You'll be bored stiff after 2 days, you'll drive your family crazy, and none of your friends will be home anyway. If you cannot design a program of study on your own (and many freshmen cannot), join a seminar or a field trip someone else has organized. Don't worry if there is nothing offered in your major field. Intersessions are great for exploring areas you don't otherwise have time to explore.

EXERCISE 4.1

In your journal, list all of your courses and the cocurricular activities you have been involved in for each one. Write for 10 minutes on how those activities have contributed to your

(continued)

Extracurricular Activities

Most colleges provide a wide variety of extracurricular events for their
students: lectures, concerts, movies, athletic events, performances,
dances, and so on. Go to some of them. You won't enjoy them all, you
won't understand everything you hear, but you will learn something
at every one. Some of these events will contribute directly to your
coursework. Attending a lecture on the ancient Greek origins of the
atomic theory, for instance, will help you in your Greek philosophy
and your introductory physics classes. Hearing a string quartet perform will help you in music appreciation. Visiting the art gallery to
look at a traveling show of nineteenth-century architectural render-
ings will help you in your studio drawing class and might also contribute to your understanding of European history.

Even the extracurricular events that seem unrelated to your coursework can be instructive. Athletic events, for instance, are mostly for
fun. But next time you watch a basketball game, think about the complex group dynamics being practiced by the ten players on the floor.
Then factor in the presence of the officials, the coaches, and the
crowd. Sociologists and psychologists spend their lifetimes studying
complex relationships such as these. Look at a long pass in a football
game in terms of vector analysis, or a gymnastics meet as an anatomy-
physiology laboratory, or a volleyball match as the playing-out of
power relationships. Every form of human endeavor is the subject of
study by some academic discipline or other. You can watch those
endeavors and be contributing, if only indirectly, to your coursework.

Jobs

Many years ago, it was relatively unusual for college students to hold
jobs. As college costs have risen and financial aid opportunities have
decreased, more and more students have been forced to find jobs so

they can go to school. Many educators regret that so many students must work. I do not. Unless a job takes so much time that there is none left for study, working will contribute to a student's education.

For most adults, working is a fact of life. We spend a large portion of our waking hours for most of our lives at work. Our jobs support us and our dependents. Many of us define ourselves through our jobs. A part-time college job can introduce students to the realities of the world of work.

How much of a job can you handle? It depends on your goals, on your abilities, and on how much energy you have. If you are headed for veterinary school, you are a competent but not brilliant student, and you need 10 hours of sleep every night, you may not have more than a few hours on weekends available for a job. In that case, I encourage you to find a job with a local vet, caring for research animals in a biology lab, or in some other setting where your work has a direct application to your studies.

At the other end of the scale, if your goal is to earn a degree of some sort with passing grades, if you are extremely bright, and if you have more energy than anyone else, you can probably handle 30 or 40 hours a week and still go to school full time. Most students fall somewhere between these extremes. Try working for 10 to 20 hours a week, and see how it goes. If you still have time to earn the grades you need to meet your goals, if exhaustion doesn't lead to illness and substandard grades, if your friends and family still speak to you, you can handle it. Otherwise, cut your hours back.

Most schools offer work–study jobs to some students who are receiving federal financial aid. If you are eligible for work–study employment, take it. You work for the college, or in some instances for an off-campus employer, in some capacity that will let you learn while you earn. The government pays most of your wages. Most schools assign eligible freshmen to work–study jobs; but after your first year you must find your own position. Look for one that will contribute as directly as possible to your academic goals. If you are pursuing an experimental science, look for a job in a lab; if you are interested in journalism, try for the newspaper; if you think you want to teach, see if the education department needs office help.

For some students, of course, having a job is not a matter of choice; it's an absolute necessity. If you are an adult returning to school or taking a few classes part time, your job probably comes first and college second. Without your job there would be no money for tuition, let alone for the necessities of life. You probably must schedule your classes around your work schedule and meet your job's responsibilities before you do your coursework. You will pay a price, of course. It is likely to take you many more years to reach your goals for going to college than it would if you could make college your first priority.

Whatever your job is, learn from it. Just finding a job is a valuable learning experience. The first time you go through the process of filling out applications, interviewing, and waiting for a decision, you may conclude that the world of work is too cold, too impersonal, too inhospitable for the likes of you. True, it is all of those things. But you're stuck in it, and the earlier you learn how to manipulate that world to your advantage, the better you will be able to handle it when you have to.

Once you have a job, there is more to learn. You must satisfy your boss, get along with your fellow workers, accommodate your work schedule to your class schedule, and conserve your energy. Learning how to do all of these things will serve you well later in life. They will also serve you well in your coursework. Many of the skills you develop in your job are also valuable in school. Satisfying a boss is not much different from satisfying an instructor. Getting along with fellow workers takes the same skills as getting along with roommates and collaborators. You must schedule your study time just as you schedule your work time, and you must make sure you have enough energy to carry out all of your school-related tasks. So learning how to work will help you learn how to go to college.

Furthermore, some of the jobs available to students can contribute to their coursework in more specific ways. Physical education majors frequently work in the field house, arranging intramural sports events, or assisting coaches. Students headed for human service professions often become floor advisers in residence halls. Education majors work as tutors; finance majors serve as local representatives for Daytona Beach motels; retailing majors sell jeans and T-shirts. If you can choose your job, try to choose one with some relation to what you are studying.

If you have no choice, do not despair. You can learn from any job, no matter how menial. Pushing hamburgers in the local fast-food franchise will teach you a great deal about organizational theory. Tending bar will show you a wide range of human behavior. Shelving books in the library will broaden your knowledge of the diversity of human intellectual activity—and besides, most librarians will let you browse a little.

If you have been working for years you have already learned most of these lessons. You know how to allocate your time, you know how to meet the expectations of the boss, you know how to make a deadline. Use that knowledge in the classroom; it gives you an enormous advantage over many of your classmates.

EXERCISE 4.2

In your journal, describe how your current (or most recent) job relates to your coursework. Does it contribute to your understanding of any of your course material? Do your job experiences give you examples you can use in class?

Now list the ways in which your job contributes to your life outside of the classroom. Do the skills your job teaches you assist you in living and working with others? Can you see ways in which your job is preparing you for life after college?

Finally, describe the part-time job that would contribute the most to your coursework and your outside-of-class life. How can you go about finding or creating that job?

Personal Relationships

Everyone has personal relationships: with parents and children, with brothers and sisters, with friends, with wives and husbands, with boyfriends and girlfriends. These relationships are essential to our well-being. They give us a network of people we can rely upon, of people who support us, of people who will talk with us and remind us when we are going astray and help us when we are desperate. Maintaining these relationships is important.

But going to college can be very hard on personal relationships. The folks who are left at home—parents, siblings, spouses, children, boy- and girlfriends—feel bereft. If you are going to a faraway school, you leave for weeks or months. Even if you are commuting, you go away every day. You set out to learn new and wonderful things, to experience all there is to experience, to meet new and exciting people. Meanwhile the folks you left at home wonder, wistfully, what you are up to. Are you abandoning them forever?

Probably not. But you will be forming new relationships at college. And the new relationships will have some effect on the ones you left at home. College is a time for exploring personal relationships, just as it is a time for exploring the curriculum and your own limitations and how society works and what makes the world go around.

Your new relationships, especially with people who are different from you, will help you learn what the world is like. People who come from different parts of the country or of the world, people who speak different languages, and people who are of different colors can teach you an enormous amount about the amazing diversity of humans. And, of course, you learn a great deal about yourself when you interact with people who are different from you.

But don't let your new relationships kill the old ones. You need those folks you left behind. They've known you the longest, they will probably still like you after you graduate, they are the best equipped to counsel you when you are lonely or depressed, and they have the resources to help you when you get in trouble. Besides, they love you and you love them; you can't afford to squander love.

Your new relationships can be stormy. They grow in an environment that is new, uncharted, and loose. No one quite knows all the rules. For instance, most new students at residential colleges assume that their roommates will be their closest friends ever. That's a good assumption to start with, because roommates must cooperate in many ways. But it seldom turns out to be true. Roommates usually have different goals, different interests, and different capacities. Sometimes those differences lead to conflicts. You may like to study from midnight until 4 A.M., sleep until 8, and catch up with a long nap in the afternoon. Your roommate may prefer a more traditional pattern. If you cannot sleep when she is studying, you are both in trouble. Floor advisers in residence halls spend large amounts of time with freshmen negotiating roommate disputes like this one.

College students frequently fall in love. That's hardly surprising. Put thousands of budding adults together in a new environment, apply fewer constraints than they had previously experienced, and many of them will fall in love. Love can be a learning experience. Just like working, loving relationships are a fact of life for most adults; college is a wonderful time to learn about them. So you will probably date, form attachments, and break attachments, sometimes with dizzying speed.*

----

*A brief note on sex. Sex—like working and love—is a fact of life for adults. As college students explore the other aspects of adult life, they will explore sex also. In past years, parents and school administrators conspired to prevent their charges from having sex. Hence single-sex colleges, limited hours for visitation, dress codes, the "one-

All of these relationships will take up some time and energy. They're worth it. We all need to be connected to other people. However, don't become so entangled in new and changing personal relationships that you have no time for the other parts of your life. Keep your goals in mind. Even if meeting new people is one of your goals, don't let the pursuit of it blind you to your other goals. Don't allow your roommate, your new boy- or girlfriend, or your new circle of pals to make your decisions for you. The peer pressure in college is intense. Most students come to college from an environment where someone else (parents, teachers, coaches, employers) decided how you will spend your time. Now that those folks have disappeared from daily view, it is tempting to let your new friends take over that decision-making role. Resist; make your own decisions.

Exercise

We all know in our minds that exercise is important. We learned about it early in school, along with the three major food groups, personal cleanliness, and drugs and alcohol. You probably haven't thought much about it since then. Most high school students are

----

foot-on-the-floor" rule, house mothers, and so on. None of these artificial structures worked very well; students still explored sex. Most of those structures have disappeared from our campuses. Few single-sex colleges remain; indeed, many residence halls are coed. Most halls have more restrictions on noise than on visits from the other sex. House mothers, dress codes, and the foot-on-the-floor rule are relics that only turn up in parents' "when *I* was in college" lectures.

Does that mean that all the problems with sex in college have disappeared? Not at all. Rape (including date rape), AIDS, and unwanted pregnancy are major concerns at most colleges today. Colleges are working hard to deal with these perils, with some success. What does that mean for you? The dangers are real. Men and women need to worry about pregnancy, about disease, about rape. (Rape victimizes women almost exclusively, but an environment in which rape occurs, especially rape by an acquaintance or a date, is unhealthy for men as well as for women.) How can you avoid them? There are no easy answers. "Just saying 'no'" will usually work, at the price of putting off that part of your adult life. If you don't always say no, take appropriate precautions: Use some form of birth control, inquire about the health of your partner, and try to avoid situations in which you might be raped. Be aware of your campus resources, such as the counseling center, women's and men's programs, clinics that test for AIDS, and pregnancy hotlines.

The key is to know what you are doing. If you do not choose to be sexually active, don't let others sway your resolve. If you do engage in sex, think about it beforehand and be cautious. But make your decisions for yourself, consciously, with some thought to the possible consequences—both good and bad.

physically active, with sports, PE, and generally running about like a teenager, so getting enough exercise was probably not an issue for you. But when you get to college, things change. You are probably not taking PE, you are probably not in intercollegiate sports, and you probably spend more time studying or sitting around than you spend running about like a teenager. All of a sudden your life is sedentary.

So what? You are entering the adult world, after all, and adults lead a pretty sedentary life, right? Why shouldn't you? Well, for several reasons. If you get a little exercise you will feel better, you will be more alert, and you will have more energy to devote to achieving your goals. Exercise is a wonderful way to reduce stress. Pounding a forehand past your opponent on the tennis court makes it a little easier to handle a C− on a quiz; grinding out a new personal record for laps in the pool helps place girl- or boyfriend problems in perspective; dominating a pickup basketball game helps make up for not dominating a discussion session. Exercise temporarily saps your physical energy, but it rebuilds mental and emotional energy.

In addition, exercise will help you counteract the dreaded "freshman 15"—the 15 pounds most freshmen add as a result of the dining hall policy of unlimited amounts of fatty and starchy foods at every meal. You can learn some things through exercise: how to set and achieve short-term goals, how to overcome apparent limitations, how to compete with yourself and others. Regular exercise is also a good habit to get into as you begin setting the patterns of behavior for your life as an adult. But these are bonuses; the most important reason to exercise is simply because it makes you feel better. And feeling better will help you work better and help you achieve your goals.

What kind of exercise should you engage in? It doesn't matter much, as long as you do it regularly. Do something that causes you to breathe hard and raise a sweat at least three times a week. But don't exhaust yourself; if you find that it takes you more than 15–20 minutes to cool down, you are doing too much at once. If you do too much at once, your exercise will become a chore instead of a recreation, and you are unlikely to continue it. You'll get much more value and satisfaction from exercising in smaller doses and more often.

Most colleges offer many opportunities for exercise: weight rooms; basketball, tennis, and racketball courts; swimming pools; tracks, paths, and trails; and so on. Most offer exercise programs: aerobics, scuba-diving instruction, orienteering, weight training, and fitness. Most residence halls have weight rooms, and some have small gyms. You may never have such opportunities again. Take advantage of them.

Many students engage in intramural sports. Wonderful, as long as you play three times a week. If you don't, supplement your intramurals with swimming, aerobics, running or walking, or something else that makes you breathe hard and that raises a sweat. Try taking an exercise break from studying instead of a snack or TV or telephone break. Study for an hour and a half, spend half an hour running or swimming or lifting weights, and then hit the books again. You'll find that your break invigorates you, relaxes you, and gives you something to be proud of. Snack breaks, TV breaks, and telephone breaks, by contrast, make you feel lazy and wasteful of your time.

Make sure your form of exercise entertains you. Some people delight in running; others find it excruciatingly boring. Some thrive on contact sports; others cringe. Experiment a little, and find the forms of exercise that revitalize you. Then build them into your schedule. Exercise should be part of your regular routine, like doing your laundry, washing your hair, going to work, and calling your mom.

EXERCISE 4.3

In your journal, list all the exercise you have gotten in the last month. Is it enough? Did it entertain you? Was it regular? Now design an exercise plan for yourself that will make you breathe hard and sweat at least three times a week, that will entertain you, and that will still leave you enough time to do everything else you must do.

Summary

Engaging yourself in your activities outside of class is as important as engaging yourself in your coursework. Your outside-of-class activities give you learning opportunities that are simply unavailable to you in class. Field trips, informal gatherings, tutoring programs, honors activities, internships, foreign study, research, and other cocurricular activities supplement your coursework in ways you cannot begin to imagine until you sample them.

Concerts, plays, exhibits, athletic events, campus politics, and other extracurricular activities will entertain you, relax you, and also supplement your coursework. Your personal relationships, exercise, and your job will sustain you emotionally, physically, and financially and will help introduce you to the adult world. And you will discover that the clear line you used to draw between work and fun has disappeared.

5

Learning with Others

───▶ **C**ollege is hard. No matter how conscientiously you have set your goals, no matter how thoroughly you have scheduled your time, no matter how aggressively you have attacked your coursework and your activities outside of class, college is still hard. There is simply a lot of studying to do, and much of it is difficult. However, there are a few techniques you can adopt to make your studying more successful. The most important is to study with others.

Collaborative Learning

What do you think about when you imagine a typical college class? A professor stands in the front of a classroom and talks; a bunch of students sit before him, silently taking notes. At the end of the hour the professor may ask for questions, and every few weeks he makes the students write an examination. But most of the time, information flows from the professor to the students. After all, he knows the most; why shouldn't he be the teacher?

Well, there are good reasons why he shouldn't always be the teacher. For one, a college is supposed to be a community of learners where faculty and students gather together to push forward the frontiers of knowledge. When the faculty is regarded

63

as the fount of information and students as empty vessels waiting to be filled, what kind of community can you have?

Secondly, when the professor always lectures and the students always listen, everyone eventually gets bored. Students fall asleep, and their instructors want to. That's why instructors ask for questions; that's why they beg students to come see them during their office hours. Talking all the time is downright boring.

But the most important reason why the professor should not always be the teacher is simply that there are better ways to learn. Remember how you learned to dance? You didn't learn through a lecture. You learned by getting up with your friends and imitating what they did, by trying some new moves to see how they worked, by practicing with your brother or best friend. You learned dancing by doing it and by paying attention to what you were doing. Was learning to dance boring? Hardly. Partly because dancing is inherently fun, partly because dancing is a socially acceptable way to interact with the other sex, partly because we dance to music we like. But mostly because you were learning *with* someone, you weren't learning *from* someone. You had a partner. You were collaborating.

EXERCISE 5.1

In your journal, list three learning experiences you have had in which you learned with a partner. Write about the advantages and disadvantages of the partnership. Finally, write about the implications of those learning activities for your college career. What lessons can you learn from them that will help you with your coursework?

Why Learn Collaboratively?

Sometimes you have a partner in college also. You may have a lab partner, a collaborator on a sociology project, or a co-researcher on a field trip. Think about what happens when you learn something with a partner. In geology lab, your instructor tells you and your lab partner to identify a particular sample of rock. First, you use your senses: You both look closely at the sample, noting its color, its shape, its grain pattern. You smell it, taste it, feel it. You experiment a little. You hit it with a hammer to see how it cleaves. Your partner applies heat to see if it melts and at what temperature. You mix it with various other substances to see how it reacts. As you make your observations, you compare perceptions to make sure that you agree. "Look at how flat it is! And I can see some light through it, can you?" "Yeah, I wonder why that is? And did you see how it peels apart?"

You consult previous knowledge. You each search back through your memories to see what minerals this stuff is similar to in your own experience. You've never seen it before, but your partner remembers seeing something like it in the door of her grandfather's wood-burning stove. "Aha," you say: You read in a book once that stove-builders used mica for little windows in the doors of wood burners because glass would melt. You check the tables of minerals in your text. After some searching you read that white mica is translucent and demonstrates one perfect cleavage. Your sample matches—eureka!

Through this process you and your partner have learned a good deal. You have learned about mica, first by examining in detail a piece of it and second by learning about its general principles in your text-book. You have also learned some of the general characteristics of minerals and the ways they are classified. Finally, you have learned one application of the scientific method: Gather data, form a hypothesis, verify it, reach a conclusion.

What good did your partner do in this process? She was an audience as you talked through your observations, and she supplied some observations of her own. The two of you together saw more in your rock sample than either of you would have on your own. Having a partner doubled the amount of experiences you could draw upon. In fact, it was her memory of her grandfather's wood-burning stove that provided a crucial clue. And having a partner doubled the research resources available to you. She could look through one set of minerals in your text while you looked through another. Could you have learned as much by yourself? You could certainly have identified your sample, though it would have taken you longer. But you would probably not have learned as much about the general characteristics of minerals or about the scientific method if you were working on your own. That's why your geology instructor makes you work with a partner.

Humans tend to learn in social contexts. Think what happens when a child learns to talk. Babies make sounds at random. Eventually they begin to imitate the sounds they hear around them. And they notice the effects the sounds they make have on the people they see. "Mama" or "dada" or whatever brings a bonus: hugs, kisses, praise. So the child says it again. And she tries some new sounds, gauges their effect, puts sounds together in new ways, tries out requests ("cookie!"), answers questions ("No!"), and so on. Before long, she talks.

Imagine how that child would learn if her parents followed the same model of education practiced in most of your classes. First, she would be subjected to several months of listening to others talk. For homework she would have to practice making those peculiar sounds —but by herself. After a few months she'd take a test to see how well she was doing. Only upon completion of the course would she be allowed to speak with others. Could she learn to talk that way? Probably. But it would take a long time, she would not talk well, and everyone would be bored stiff.

Collaborative learning—learning with others—is a very natural process. We all do it, all the time. Sometimes your instructors will encourage you to learn collaboratively in your classes. Sometimes they won't. But even when they don't, there are many ways you can still learn collaboratively.

STUDY GROUPS

Is there a course that's particularly difficult for you? Or one that you simply must do well in for your major, or your program, or to keep your dad or your spouse off your back? You should form a study group for that course. Ask a few students who are taking the same course with you if they would like to study together. Keep your group small; three or four is ideal. Meet regularly, two or three times a week for an hour.

If you know your own learning style (see Chapter 3), try to form a group with students whose learning styles complement yours. Generally speaking, splitters like to work together; lumpers do not. But a group of splitters can profit from recruiting at least one congenial lumper to provide theoretical frames for the detail the splitters provide. And a group of lumpers can benefit from a splitter or two who can help them bring their theories down to earthbound applications. Visual learners and auditory learners have much to teach each other. No matter what your learning style, be tolerant of styles that differ from yours. Remember that you are all in this together and that you all can learn from one another.

Within your study group you should summarize for each other the major points in the readings and lecture, explain difficult points to the confused, invent possible exam questions and their answers, and encourage each other. Use your pencils. If you don't write things down, your study group may have a tendency to degenerate into social gatherings. (There's nothing wrong with social gatherings, but this is study time, remember?)

Each of you should bring to the meeting a short written list of what you want to accomplish in the meeting that day. Devote the first few minutes to reviewing your lists and agreeing on an agenda. You might decide to spend 15 minutes listing the major points of Chapter 7, 10 minutes summarizing the last two lectures, and half an hour generating test questions and answers.

To list the major points of Chapter 7, each of you should write down the three most important points. Then everyone should share the lists, argue them out, and negotiate an agreement on what the basic concepts of the chapter are. Use the same trick to summarize the lectures. You will learn very quickly that even when your mind seems empty, having to list things on paper will help stimulate your memory and your reasoning powers.

Use the same technique to generate exam questions. If each of you writes five exam questions, shares them, and then writes five more, you will have a list of questions covering at least 90 percent of the material your instructor has covered. And if you sketch what an appropriate answer to each question will look like, you will all be a long way toward being ready for the exam. All you need to do is review your notes from class, from your reading, and from your study group meetings; go over the exam questions your group came up with and prepare complete answers to them; and get a good night's sleep.

Make sure that each member of the group participates. None of you is the professor; each of you is a learner. Sometimes one of you will understand a particular section better than everyone else, or someone will consistently give the clearest explanations. Nonetheless, insist that everyone contribute something. Persons who are left out will no longer feel part of the group; their minds will wander, they will lose that exciting sense of participation and discovery, and they will stop learning.

Law students frequently form study groups to help them master the enormous amounts of information they must turn into usable knowledge. Typically, they will meet together nightly. Each member will take responsibility for understanding and summarizing a particular case or legal principle; in their group meetings they share what they have learned. That's probably more structure than you need, but if you are taking a course that requires mastery of huge amounts of information, try it.

Study groups take advantage of many of the basic principles you have learned elsewhere in this book. In a study group you are actively engaged in your own learning while you are pursuing your goals. A study group forces you to use language; you must speak and write about the concepts most important to the course, thus cementing them in your memory. And in a study group you can take advantage of the learning styles of others as well as your own.

Is it cheating? Not at all. In fact you might let your instructor know that you are in a study group, identify the members, and ask him for some suggestions on what you should spend your time on. He will be impressed with your initiative and zeal, and he may give you some old tests or lecture notes to help you. The only time anyone will think a study group is cheating is if the answers you produce on an essay test are absolutely identical. If your group is learning together your answers may be similar, but they will not be identical.

EXERCISE 5.2

In your journal, invent a study group for one of your courses. List the members you would like to recruit. (Caution: Don't automatically choose your pals. Groups composed of pals frequently fail; you tend to spend your time visiting and chatting and being pals, rather than studying.) Write an agenda for your first meeting. Now do it: Recruit a group, meet, and study together.

WRITING PROJECTS

In many of your classes you will have to write papers or essays. For most of us, these are tough assignments. Getting started is usually the toughest part. Talking about your essay with another person can be enormously helpful. You don't need a study group or a written agenda; you only need an audience so you can do your thinking out loud.

"My English comp instructor wants me to write about the most significant experience in my life. What's a significant experience? I guess it's something that happened to me that made a difference, that had an impact. Like the time I drove the car into the lake; I've had nightmares ever since, and I'm still afraid to drive at night. I guess I can write about that."

In this case your partner contributed nothing but an ear. That's not nothing; it takes the presence of an ear to stimulate most of us to pursue a line of thought. (Sometimes you can simulate the presence of an ear by writing in your journal. Try it if there is no ear available.) In other cases your partner will contribute a lot: a trial definition of "significant," an idea for his paper that sparks two ideas in you, a suggestion that you connect your two ideas in a certain way, and so on.

Once you have started on your essay, don't abandon your partner. Show him an outline, if you have one, or your rough draft. Ask for his reaction. Do the same for him. You should each be careful not to offend. Always begin your reaction with a positive comment: "This is a really good topic, and your lead sentence sets it up well." But offer constructive criticism as well: "I don't see the point of the third paragraph; what exactly are you trying to say there?" Be specific. "This is good, but I think you can do better" is not helpful. Use the techniques of criticism that you are learning in your composition class.

You and your partner can also serve as final proofreaders for each other. Check spelling, punctuation, capitalization, grammar, and so on for correctness. Don't make the corrections on your partner's paper. Point them out, ask if that is really correct, and let him decide what to do about it.

We were all taught as children that writing is a lonely activity. But almost no one writes entirely alone. Your instructors certainly do not. Most academic writing, especially in the sciences and social sciences, is done jointly from beginning to end. Most journal articles in those fields have several authors; some have ten or fifteen! Even when a professor is the sole author, she will typically discuss her project with colleagues, circulate drafts for comment, and read preliminary versions at conferences before producing the final version. So even if your instructor does not encourage you to write papers with a partner, do it anyway. If it works for you—that is, if your papers turn out well and earn good grades—let your instructor know how you did it. Most will be impressed; some may even build your technique into subsequent courses.

JOINT RESEARCH

In some of your courses you will do research projects. In sociology you might take a survey of the residents of a neighborhood; in geology you might try to date the strata of rock in a local quarry; in chemistry you might analyze the differences between the water supplied by two nearby towns. Professors love to assign research projects; they are wonderful tools for learning.

Research projects are perfect vehicles for collaboration. Frequently they are designed for pairs; the first part of the assignment is to choose a partner. Sometimes your instructor will not build partners into the design. When that happens, ask if you can do the project jointly. She may say yes, but only if you double the size of the project. Do it. Having a partner is worth doubling the project.

What are the advantages? Two persons working together have a much better chance of thinking of all the variables, asking the right questions, and avoiding the dead ends than one person working alone. That's why detectives work in pairs and why most practicing researchers work in groups. You and your partner should start by agreeing on your goals for the research and the steps you will take to get there. If both of you are going off in different directions or getting in each other's way, your project is likely to fail. On the other hand, if you are heading in the same direction with the same agenda, you'll reinforce each other's work. You may find that dividing the chores between you works well, as long as each of you understands how your partner's tasks fit into the research design.

Both of you must contribute approximately equally to the project. If one person does all the work, the other gets annoyed. Frequently that annoyance is transmitted to the instructor, resulting in a poor grade. Worse, the person who does no work learns nothing. And if you are learning nothing, why spend your time and money on the course in the first place?

TUTORING PROGRAMS

Most colleges have a tutoring program of some sort. Some have a centralized tutoring program in a learning center that will provide you with a tutor in any course you are taking; some have departmental tutors who sit in offices waiting for students to drop in for help in biology or English composition; some have tutors for particular groups of students, such as athletes or minority students or premeds. Whatever sort of programs your college provides, take advantage of it. Tutoring programs offer you wonderful opportunities for collaborative learning.

If the tutoring program your school offers is one-on-one—that is, one tutor per tutee—your tutor is your collaborator. Your tutor can be the audience you need to work through an essay, your partner in figuring out the steps to follow in solving a calculus problem, or your fellow researcher in deciphering nineteenth-century census data for your history class.

You must make sure that you and your tutor have a collaborative relationship. Some tutors like to think of themselves as junior professors whose function is to lecture to you, to solve your math problems for you, to do your research for you. They are not likely to be very helpful. (After all, the reason you're in tutoring is because you didn't quite get the point of the lecture; another lecture isn't going to do much more than put you to sleep.) Insist that your tutor act more like a fellow learner; if she won't, complain to your tutor coordinator.

Some tutoring programs set up tutoring groups instead of one-to-one partnerships. Groups work well, as long as they are no larger than five or six. In a tutoring group the tutor acts as a facilitator, helping the tutees learn. Sometimes two tutees will work together on a problem, with an occasional visit from the tutor; other times the tutor will ask a question of the group as a whole and let them work out the answer together. Once again, the key to making a tutoring group work for you is to treat it as a collaborative learning experience. You should become actively involved in the workings of the group, and you should not let the tutor act like a professor.

Some students, especially new freshmen, think that using a tutor is shameful. "I can do it on my own," they tell their advisers; "I'm not a dummy." True, you're not a dummy. But you're probably not brilliant in everything, either. Most students are strong in some areas, weaker in others. In your weak areas, you can profit from some assistance. The very best colleges and universities have tutoring programs, and the very best students use them. So don't be ashamed.

You should also think about becoming a tutor. The best way to learn something is to teach it to someone else; that's one reason collaborative learning works. Tutors frequently report that they learn more than their tutees. Most programs hire students who have been successful in the courses they will tutor. ("Successful" means Bs or As. B students frequently make better tutors than A students. They seem to have a better appreciation for the struggles students must go through to understand material that is difficult for them.)

EXERCISE 5.3

Find out what sort of tutoring program your college offers, where it is located, and how you can use it. Request tutoring for the course that is most difficult for you. After your first session, write for 5 minutes in your journal about what worked and what didn't work in the tutoring session.

CO- AND EXTRACURRICULAR PROJECTS

In the last chapter you read about the wonderful learning opportunities available to you outside of the classroom. Most of what you learn outside the classroom is learned collaboratively. When you and your roommate figure out how to build a loft in your room, you learn together about designing a stable structure, buying lumber, and negotiating with your resident adviser. When your club puts on a dance, you learn together about organizing an event, purchasing food, and hanging decorations. When your residence hall governing body decides to punish underage drinkers, you learn together how the political process works.

Take advantage of those instances of collaborative learning outside the classroom. Pay attention to them, watch how you learn, and then apply the same learning techniques to your schoolwork. If you and your roommate learned how to build your loft by joint trial and error ("Try nailing this piece over there. Whoops! Okay, use a bolt instead"), try working your algebra problems with him in the same way ("Let's try this. Whoops! Okay, I guess we have to factor first").

If you and your club members succeed by delegating tasks, try the same trick with your research team. If you and your governing body can only reach consensus by agreeing to settle the issues before dawn and then arguing for hours, try writing a practice test with your study group by setting a time limit and then arguing out the most likely questions. If a learning technique works with co- and extracurricular projects, it will work anywhere.

Summary

Learning with others is frequently the best and fastest way to learn. You can learn with others—collaboratively—in a variety of ways: in study groups and tutoring programs, in research projects and extracurricular activities. Some of your instructors will encourage you, perhaps even require you, to learn collaboratively; others will not. But you can practice collaborative learning techniques no matter what your instructors say.

CHAPTER 6

Remembering and Reproducing What You Learn

Over the years, many students have come to me after failing an exam, saying "I knew all of that stuff yesterday, really, I studied so hard—I just couldn't remember it on the test!" Some were exaggerating, I'm sure, but most were not. They really did understand the material while studying, but lost it during the exam. Perhaps that's happened to you.

This chapter will show you in a brief and somewhat superficial way how your memory works, how you can improve it, and how you can put that memory to work when you are taking examinations.

How Memory Works

Psychologists tell us that memory is the capacity to store and retrieve information. Memory consists of three different systems: sensory memory, short-term memory, and long-term memory.* Normally when we think of memory we think of

---

*Actually, psychologists disagree to some extent about this distinction. Some say that there are three entirely different components of memory; others say that memory is one structure with several different ways of working. But all psychologists agree that we can clearly distinguish between the ways sensory memory, short-term memory, and long-term memory work. That's enough for the purposes of this book. If you would like to know more about memory, consult one or both of these books: A. Baddely, *Your Memory: A User's Guide,* NY, Macmillan, 1982; E. Loftus, *Memory,* Reading, MA, Addison-Wesley, 1980. Or take a psychology course.

remembering information for days, weeks, months, years—that's long-term memory. But we wouldn't have any long-term memories if we didn't have short-term memories to feed them, and we wouldn't have any short-term memories if we had no sensory memories.

Sensory memory is the almost instantaneous memory you have of the information your senses give you. When you look out the window, for instance, you see the building across the street: two-story red brick facade, windows with white trim and shutters, person coming through the door, grass, trees, and so on. That image is implanted in your sensory memory. Sensory memory is fleeting; that image will last less than a second, to be replaced by another image supplied by your eyes. The image does not disappear forever; it is stored in your short-term memory.

Short-term memories last only for a minute or so. If someone comes into your room and asks you what you were just looking at, you could probably list some of what you saw. Five minutes later, you could not; your short-term memories from your glance out the window are already gone. When you look up a number in the telephone book, you store it in short-term memory. That memory lasts long enough for you to dial, and then you forget it.

A seven- or ten-digit phone number is about as much as our short-term memories can handle. When someone asks you a question while you are dialing the number you just looked up, your short-term memory becomes overloaded and you forget the number. If, for some reason, a phone number (or an image, or an important date, or anything else) is worth remembering, you store it in your long-term memory, where it might last forever (or until you die, whichever comes first).

Most of the information we store in our short-term memories is not preserved. Imagine how cluttered our memories would be if we remembered everything we ever saw, heard, and smelled. We'd never have the time or the capacity to think about anything—all of our mental space would be occupied by old images. We preserve short-term memories only if we have some reason to do so. If you recognize the person coming out of the house across the street as your close friend, for instance, you will probably store that bit of information away in your long-term memory. But you are not likely to store the fact that three windows are open or that the grass needs cutting unless you have some special interest in windows or grass.

How long will you remember that your close friend came through her door while you happened to be glancing out your window on this particular day? It all depends on how important this event turns out

Figure 6.1 *The structure of memory*

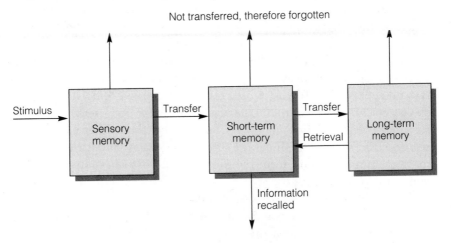

to be. If she turns away from the door and is run over by a bus before your horrified eyes, chances are you will remember that image for a very long time. You'll dredge the image out of long-term memory to tell the awful tale to your friends later that day, to your classmates when you return for reunions, and to your grandchildren when you are warning them about crossing the street.

On the other hand, if nothing extraordinary happens, you'll probably forget it as soon as you ask her where she was going. If an image is important to us for some reason or other, we'll reinforce it by thinking about it every now and again, and it will stay with us for a long time. If it's not important, it will fade away fairly quickly.

The structure of memory is depicted in Figure 6.1. In the example given earlier, the stimulus is your vision of the scene across the street. The sensory memory is the visual image your senses give you. That image is stored in your short-term memory for a minute or two and then dumped, unless you have some reason to remember it—such as her immediate demise. In that case, it is stored in your long-term memory. When you want to recall it to tell the lurid details to your friends or your grandchildren, you bring it back to short-term memory so that you have access to it.

Computers serve as a useful analogue to human memory. Sensory memory is like the keystrokes you make to show characters on the screen. Short-term memory is like the computer's random-access memory, and long-term memory is like the computer's disk storage. When you are writing a paper for English on your old Apple® II, the keystrokes you enter produce images of letters on the screen, just the way your vision produces images in your sensory memory. Those letters (and the English paper they eventually turn into) are held in the computer's memory for a (relatively) short period of time—until you turn off the machine. Similarly, your sensory memories are held in your short-term memory for a (very) short period of time. But if you save your paper in a file on a disk, you can preserve it indefinitely, just as you can transfer your short-term memories to long-term memory for preservation. When you want to work on that paper again, you retrieve the file into the machine's memory, just as you retrieve information from your long-term memory into short-term memory when you want to reminisce.

There are differences between human memory and computers, of course. Computers are somewhat faster at storing and retrieving information, by most measures, but humans can process more information at the same time. (Humans use what computer scientists call "parallel processors"—that is, we can think about lots of things at the same time. Most computers have only one processor, so they can only do one chore at a time.) One of the most glaring differences is that, compared to humans, computers have an enormous amount of short-term memory. Your old Apple® II probably can store 64,000 characters at one time in its random-access memory; newer personal computers can store as many as 64 million characters. And computers can hold on to all of those memories as long as they are turned on. Most humans, by contrast, can store no more than ten items in short-term memory at a time, and for no more than a minute or so.

On the other hand, humans can store far more information in long-term memory than any computer yet built, or even conceived. Think of everything you know: hundreds of places, thousands of faces, as many as 100,000 words, millions of objects, uncountable experiences. Psychologists estimate that adults possess somewhere around a septillion bits of information—1,000,000,000,000,000,000,000,000 items. That's a lot. Combine our huge storage with our parallel processors and we can outperform any computer there is, at least on human-type tasks—eating grapes while cleaning the refrigerator while listening to the ball game while thinking about a philosophy assignment and wondering if our sweethearts really love us. Of course computers can beat us at a few tasks: counting without losing track, remembering with precision, solving complicated equations.*

----

*For an interesting discussion of the mind analyzed as if it were a computer, see M. Minsky, *The Society of Mind*, NY, Simon & Schuster, 1985.

So who cares how your memory works, and how much information it can hold, and how it compares to computers? You do. Without a memory that works well, you cannot succeed as a student. As you read your texts, as you listen to lectures, as you gather data in labs, you are filling your sensory memory registers, then transferring images to short-term memory, and finally storing some of that information in your long-term memory. When you study for the exam, you are recalling information from your short-term memory, reinforcing it, and storing it once again in long-term memory. When you actually take the test you are dredging the information out of long-term memory once again, storing it briefly in short-term memory, and then spitting it out onto the test. If your memory systems break down somewhere along the line, you fail the test.

Improving Your Memory

All of us know a great deal about how our memories work, even if we don't know the differences among sensory, short-term, and long-term memory. We know that we tend to forget what we see and hear unless we pay attention. We know that we remember the things that are most important to us. We know that repeating things helps us remember them for long periods of time. But knowing how memory works helps you understand those phenomena.

PAYING ATTENTION

Consider again what happens when you look out the window at the building across the street. Your sensory memory records whatever your eyes see and transfers it into short-term memory. Your short-term memory can only hold a few items at a time, and so it tends to dump them out quickly. Unless you are paying attention for some reason, that information is likely to disappear forever. But if you are paying attention to what you see—say, because you are sketching it for your drawing class—then you will transfer the information to your long-term memory. And then it's available to you for quite a while, at least. In other words, one of the ways to make sure that information gets transferred from short-term to long-term memory is to pay attention to it.

You already knew that, of course. You have to pay attention in class, or reading your texts, or in lab in order to remember anything.

But now you know why: If you don't attend to the bits of information in short-term memory, you dump them out to nowhere, never to be seen—or recalled—again. How do you make yourself pay attention, especially when you find the class material boring or confusing or irrelevant? If it's boring, take notes (you'll learn more about note taking in Part II). If it's confusing, treat it like a puzzle you must solve, and do whatever you have to do to solve it (once again, Part II will tell you more). If it seems irrelevant, make it relevant by drawing a clearer connection between the class and your own goals.

ATTENDING TO WHAT'S IMPORTANT

Why should you pay attention to those bits of information you are getting from the lecture, or your text, or your experiment, and not to others? You are receiving other bits of information as well, after all, from your other senses; why not pay attention to the information they send streaming through your short-term memory? You do attend to those other bits of information, of course, at least to a degree. If your feet hurt from playing too much basketball you will always be barely aware of the pain, and if you are worried about your child in the day care center you will not be able to completely suppress your concern. But what will you store in your long-term memory? If you are concentrating on your schoolwork, you'll ignore most of the pain and the worry, and most of the other information streaming through short-term memory, and store only what's relevant to the class.

How do you do that? By deciding beforehand what's important to you, for instance by completing the goal-setting exercises of Chapter 1. And by reminding yourself from time to time what your goals are and that feeling the pain from your feet or worrying about your child are not going to help you meet them. You can't completely control how your mind works; sometimes pain or worry becomes too distracting to ignore. But you can decide what is most important to you. If you work at reminding yourself about your list of priorities, your memory will follow your instructions most of the time. Or at least enough of the time to earn you decent grades.

REPEATING TO REMEMBER

You learned at an early age that repeating something over and over helped you remember it. Now you know why that happens. Repeating the lyrics of a song, for instance, means transferring the words

Figure 6.2 *The forgetting curve* (Adapted from original research by H. Eddinghaus in 1885, reproduced in A. Baddely, *Your Memory: A User's Guide*, NY, Macmillan, 1982, page 47)

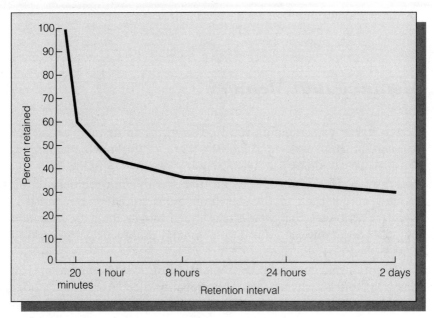

from long-term memory to short-term memory, saying them, and then storing them again in long-term memory. This process refreshes and reinforces your memory.

Figure 6.2 depicts the forgetting curve; it shows how memory fades. Twenty minutes after learning something, you can only remember 60 percent of it. After an hour you've lost more than half; after 8 hours you remember less than 40 percent. The more time passes, the more you forget. But every time you bring something from long-term memory to short-term memory and then re-store it, you restart the clock. The result is that you remember more of the material for a longer period of time.

Note that it is virtually impossible to remember 100 percent of anything. But no one wants to do that. If you remembered 100 percent of your history lecture, for instance, your memory would be impossibly cluttered with all of your weird professor's "ahems" and "umms," with the gum-snapping of the guy next to you, with the rumbling of your own stomach, with the feel of the sunshine on your arm, with the daydream that distracted you for a few moments, and so on. You filter out most of that before it even gets to long-term memory. But even what gets to long-term memory will soon fade unless you bring it back from time to time. That's the second reason why you take notes: to help you reinforce your memory. (The first, remember, is to help you pay attention.)

Meaning and Memory

How is it that your memory can find anything in its vast storehouse? Suppose someone asks you when the battle of Yorktown was fought. You learned all about the Revolutionary War in high school, so you instantly say 1781. How did you do that? Surely your memory didn't search through each of the septillion items stored therein until it found "Yorktown"; that would take much longer than the second it took for you to answer, even if your mental processors were working at the speed of light.

Imagine your memory as a giant filing system, one that you mostly invented on your own. You probably filed "Yorktown" under "Battles of the Revolutionary War," which is filed under "U.S. History," which is filed under "Courses Taken in High School," and so on. Alternatively, you might have filed "Yorktown" under "Cities in Virginia," under "Last Summer's Trip," under "Vacations with the Family." Or you may have some completely different filing system. And it doesn't stop there, of course. Under "Yorktown" you have probably filed other information, such as "Defeat of the British," "Cornwallis," and "French Fleet."

Sometimes you can catch flashes of your own filing system as you try to retrieve a bit of information. Or you can listen as a friend tries to recall something by running through a string of associations: "Let's see, you wanted to know the name of the third person on the right, bottom row, of my sixth-grade class picture. Sixth grade, that was Miss Snyder, there she is with her hair in a bun. And my best friend was Lee, standing there next to me. And his twin sister, standing over here, knew that person—I remember going to a birthday party, October it was, at her house, her mother made the best cake, Mrs. Donohue, that's it! Ellen Donohue." Filing systems do not always seem logical to someone else, but if they work, who cares?

Without your filing system, your memory would be just a jumble of unrelated information, very little of which you could ever retrieve. Your system connects one bit to the next, which connects it to another, and so on, so that you can find most bits sooner or later if you keep working at it. Many bits are connected in several ways; you might come to the battle of Yorktown through many different routes, especially if you have lots of information in your memory about either the Revolutionary War or the geography of Virginia.

Your filing system, your way of connecting all of the bits of information in your memory, is your network of meaning. The phrase "battle of Yorktown" has meaning for you because it is connected in your memory to an entire matrix of dates, names, events, and consequences. The red plastic shovel you come across while cleaning the basement has meaning for you because you remember hitting your little brother with it at the beach when you were 6. An equation in chemistry has meaning for you because you remember how to solve it. Without those meanings—without the filing system—you remember nothing.

Consequently, in order to remember anything you must invest it with meaning. It is extremely difficult to remember things that mean nothing to you. Memorize this string of letters: ntowhcpog etuwuest. Now close your eyes and try to remember them. You failed, right? Everyone does. Yet you know as many as a hundred thousand strings of letters—words—and can reproduce them instantly, on demand. The difference is that words have meaning for you; random strings of letters do not.

What does this mean for your life as a student? It means that you shouldn't bother trying to memorize stuff that means nothing to you; it won't work. Instead, give it some meaning. Place it in a context, connect it to some other bits of information in your memory, associate it with something already meaningful to you. You will find it much easier to remember information that is meaningful.

Many students taking a required math or science course think they can pass if they just memorize enough. Wrong. Memorizing a bunch of equations or formulas without understanding what they mean and how they are used is almost as impossible as memorizing nonsense strings of letters. The best way to pass those courses is to work with those equations or formulas enough that you understand what they mean. If you have performed the experiments that produce the formulas, for example, you'll remember them for a long time.

The next best way is to understand at least what they are used for. You will find it easy to remember the rate of acceleration of a falling body, for instance, if you have imagined yourself as a skydiver. If you have derived limits for physics problems, you'll remember those equations for calculus. At the very least, understand how to manipulate the equations and formulas: "I don't know where this equation comes from or who would ever use something like this, but I know how to solve it; $x = 24$." If you know how to solve it, the equation is connected in at least that way to a network of meanings in your long-term memory and is probably retrievable.

Learning a foreign language entails memorizing lots of new words. But note that you start with simple nouns, words that stand for objects or colors or numbers. Your instructor is making things as easy as possible for you. By starting with "un" for "one," "bleu" for "blue," "homme" for "man," and so on, he is making it easy for you to connect these foreign words to bits of information that are readily accessible in your long-term memory. You use "one," "blue," and "man" so frequently that they are connected in numerous ways to hundreds of other words, concepts, and images in your memory bank. One more connection—to a French word—is relatively easy to add. After a little while you'll add verbs and adjectives to your vocabulary; their primary connection will be to their equivalent words in English. Eventually you'll learn words that are quite abstract and that are connected in not very many ways at all to existing items in your memory. The trick with them is to do whatever you can to multiply the number of connections, such as using the words in a variety of disparate sentences, for instance.

If, for some reason, you simply cannot understand the network of meanings behind something, you can always create one. If you have to remember $E = mc^2$, for instance, but you don't have time to learn the general theory of relativity, you might connect it to a sentence you make up: "Every man's cows come," or "Everyday equals much common courtesy." Some premed students entertain themselves by making up sentences like these to stand for the long strings of carbon molecules they have to learn for organic chemistry. They find it a wonderful way of preparing for exams. Of course it encourages them to work with those formulas in their short-term memory, which has the benefit of reinforcing them in long-term memory and making them accessible for recall on the test.

Aids to Memory

There are some tricks you can use that might improve your memory. Don't spend a lot of time trying to develop these skills. By far the best way to improve your memory is to improve your understanding of the material; the more ways the information is connected to other bits of information in your long-term memory, the more accessible it is. Nonetheless, these devices may help you.

CHUNKING

If you have to learn a large block of material, the first thing to do is to divide it into manageable segments, or chunks. Each chunk is much easier to remember than an enormous string. Remember that your short-term memory has a capacity of only a handful of items. Consequently your chunks of material should be no longer than the maximum amount your short-term memory can handle: six or seven for most people.

Next, find some way to connect the chunks so you can reproduce the totality if you have to. You might assign a letter to each of the chunks and string the letters together into a word or a sentence. (That's why we invent acronyms; "NATO" is easier to remember, say, and write than "North Atlantic Treaty Organization.") For years students have used the sentence "Men Very Easily Make Jugs Serve Useful and Numerous Purposes" to remember the order of the planets (Mercury, Venus, Earth, Mars, Jupiter, Saturn, Uranus, Neptune, Pluto). In this case, the first letter of each word (except "and") stands for the first letter of a planet. Studies show that some students remember material better if they chunk it and use some sort of code like this, especially if they make up the codes themselves.

If you can invent a string of words or a sentence that rhymes, it will be far easier to remember. (Rhyming is a wonderful aid to memory. Some historians of language claim that plays used to be written in verse so that the players could memorize them easily, even though they had no printed texts.) How many days are there in March? Most of us answer that question by reciting "Thirty days hath September . . ." Premed students learn to remember the difference between cyanates, which are harmless, and cyanides, which are very poisonous, by learning "-ate I ate; -ide I died."

VISUALIZING

When someone asks you to name the first thirteen states of the Union, what do you do? If you imagine a map of the United States and start naming the original ones, you have a good visual memory. You can make good use of it in your classwork.

Much of the material you must learn is already visual material. In social science classes some of the information you need to remember is tied to maps; in science classes you must be able to duplicate diagrams; in foreign language classes you must remember lists of words. If you have a good visual memory, you should be able to reproduce those items without much difficulty. You can improve your ability to remember visually organized material by making a few maps or diagrams or lists yourself; you'll find that the repetition helps cement them in your long-term memory.

Even if the material you wish to remember is not in a map or diagram or list, you can sometimes recast it in visual form. In Part II you will learn a technique to transform written material into a map of concepts. If you have a good visual memory, the map is easy to recall when you need the information on an exam. Or sometimes you can create a visual image that represents what you need to remember. The Spanish word for horse is "caballo" (pronounced "cob-EYE-yo"); you might remember it by storing the image of a horse kicking you in the eye.

▶ EXERCISE 6.1 ◀

Pick your most boring class, the one in which it's almost impossible to remember what the instructor says. Write in your journal three ways you can improve your memory for those deadly lectures. Now put at least one of those three ways into practice.

Reproducing What You Know on Exams

So now you know a little about how your memory works; how can that knowledge help you do better on your quizzes, tests, and exams?

THE VALUE OF REPETITION

The forgetting curve (Figure 6.2) demonstrates that your memories slowly fade away unless they are refreshed. The trick is to recall them from long-term memory into short-term memory, use them, and then re-store them. Does that mean that you have to reread every text every day or every week? Tape your lectures and listen to them over and over? Redo your lab experiments? Not at all. You need only review, briefly, the main points of your reading, your lectures, and your labs. Remember how long-term memory works. Each bit of information is connected to other bits of information in a network of meaning. If you recall a major concept in that network, the other items tend to come along with it.

For example, suppose yesterday's lecture in Introduction to Computer Science was about top-down program design (creating an overall design for your program before you create the details). You understood it pretty well and took good notes. But now it's 24 hours later; according to the forgetting curve, more than half of that lecture is already gone. But if you look over your notes, even if only for a few minutes, you'll find that the rest comes back to you easily. The investment of those few minutes has restored 80 or 90 percent of the material in your memory. You've reset the clock on the forgetting curve.

You've also strengthened the connections between those bits of information by recalling them. Whenever you recall information, you think about it. You might muse that top-down program design is a lot like planning a vacation trip in advance, or speculate for a moment or two about how the advent of top-down programming affected the development of software for personal computers. Those thoughts might seem irrelevant to you at the time; you might even have to snap yourself back to your notes for fear of being distracted. But those thoughts are helping you strengthen the network of meanings within which the information you have to remember nestles in your long-term memory. And the stronger that network is, the more ways the different bits of information are connected to what you already know. The more connections there are in your memory, the easier it is to remember the material on an exam.

You'll learn several different study techniques that take advantage of the value of repetition in Part II. Basically, the trick is to recall the material often, but briefly. Some students spend half an hour every evening reviewing the day's lecture and reading notes. Others spend those wasted minutes before class starts looking over their notes from the previous day or looking through the chapter they've just read. Still others spend a few hours every weekend thoroughly reviewing the week's work. These students find that they seldom need to spend long hours studying for exams; they've done their studying long in advance by periodically reviewing their notes.

STUDYING IN BRIEF SPURTS

You may already have noticed that you study better in half-hour- or hour-long blocks than you study for 2 or 3 uninterrupted hours. This is partly because of your attention span; few of us can concentrate successfully for more than 30 or 40 minutes. But psychologists have also learned that you remember more if you divide your study time into short blocks with a brief break between them.

Suppose you try to remember a list of things you need at the store: butter, eggs, cola, bread, cheese, potato chips, shampoo, pickles, ground beef, tuna fish. Chances are you will remember the first few items and the last few, but forget at least some of the ones in the middle. You'll remember the first few because they went into long-term memory almost immediately; psychologists call this the "primacy effect." You'll remember the last few because they were the last ones entered into short-term memory and nothing came after to displace them; consequently they were successfully stored in long-term memory as well. Psychologists call this the "recency effect." If you tested how well a group of people could remember the various items on a list like this and graphed the results, it would look like Figure 6.3. Most people would remember the first item and the last item, but fewer would remember the items in the middle.

When you study, you are most likely to remember the first few items you studied and the last few. The first items you study will likely make it into long-term memory as the beneficiary of the primacy effect; the last few will profit from the recency effect. If you study for 2 or 3 hours at a time, you will successfully store away what you study first and what you study last, but you are likely to forget much of what you study in the middle. So the trick is to shrink the middle. If you study for shorter blocks of time, you'll have less "middle" material to forget; consequently you'll remember more.

MAKING YOUR OWN
CONNECTIONS

The best way to remember something is to invest it with lots of meaning. When you give an item meaning, you multiply the connections between it and other items in your long-term memory. The more connections, the easier it is to retrieve it.

How do you invest an item with lots of meaning? Some of the things you study should already be extremely meaningful. If you are

Figure 6.3 *The primacy and recency effects* (Adapted from E. Loftus, *Memory,* Reading, MA, Addison-Wesley, 1980, page 25)

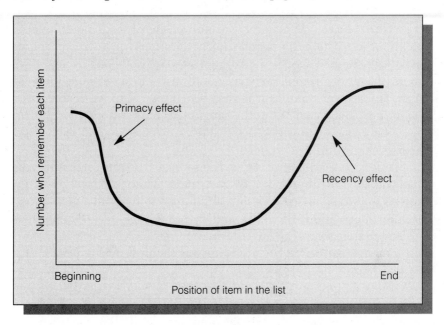

absolutely determined to go to medical school, the details of anatomy and physiology should be extremely important to you. Consequently the material you learn for Introduction to Biology should be very meaningful. Chances are you learned much of it in high school, so the basic structures are already in your memory, thoroughly connected to other bits of information. And your determination to do well in such a crucial course for your major should add considerable meaning: If you don't do well in this course, you'll never get into med school.

But with much—perhaps most—of the items you study, your ambition will not be enough; you'll have to find some other ways to invest them with meaning. The basic trick is simply to work with the material. Study it often, and study in small blocks of time. Every time you drag those bits of information out of storage, think about them a little, and put them back again, you are strengthening the old connections and building new ones.

Organized review   Get together with two or three other students from your class a few days before the exam to study together. First, list the most important topics. Second, review the most important points under each topic. Third, go off and study them. Reconvene the night before the exam for a final review.

Practice tests   Whenever you are reviewing your notes—daily, weekly, or just before the exam—invent questions the instructor might ask. Write them down in the margin of your notebook. A few days before the exam, transcribe your questions onto a separate piece of paper, and answer them as if it were a real test. Make it as accurate a simulation as you can: Write the same types of questions your professor is likely to ask (multiple choice, short answer, essay, and so on), and impose a time limit on yourself.

The test you write will not be the same as the one your professor gives you, but it will probably be fairly close. More important, writing answers to those practice questions will force you to recall and manipulate the information. Recalling and manipulating it will strengthen and add to the meanings that information has for you. As a result you will remember it better when you answer the professor's questions on the real exam.

A final suggestion: Write practice tests in your organized review session. When writing questions for yourself, you will sometimes ignore the areas you don't understand very well. But the professor won't, so you need to find a way to prepare for those questions as well as the ones on material you understand clearly. Answering practice questions written by someone else will help ensure that you cover all areas.

CRAMMING FOR EXAMS

Is cramming a good idea? Is it worth your while to ignore your books until the night before the exam and then study like crazy, usually all night long? No. You won't perform nearly as well on the exam as you would if you had reviewed the material all along, in brief spurts. Still, there will come a time when you have two choices: Cram or don't study at all. If those are your only choices, cram. But remember how your memory works, and cram so that you maximize your chances to remember as much as possible.

First, be selective. You can't possibly memorize everything that has happened in class since the last exam, so don't even try. Figure out what is most important, and concentrate on that. How do you know what's most important? You should have the evidence readily at hand in your class notes. Most instructors lecture about what they think is most important in a course. If you've been taking notes in class, they are probably a reliable guide. Other students in the class can also give you a good indication of what's important. Sometimes the instructor will tell you; the day before the exam, ask what sorts of questions are likely to be on the test or what material the test will cover. The worst she can do is laugh at your bravado.

Once you know which concepts are most important, concentrate on them. Read enough of your text to ensure that you understand them, and summarize what you have read in your own words. Write down some examples; you might find a few in the text, or buried in your notes, or perhaps you can make up a few. Examples are important; on an essay exam, an illustrative example can convince the instructor that you know what you're talking about, even if you can't quite say it. Finally, make up a few practice questions about the material you have reviewed, and write answers to them. Writing practice questions and answers will force you to drag the material out of long-term memory, manipulate it a little, and store it again. When you see questions on the exam calling for that material, it will come forward more easily as a result of your practice.

Accept the fact that you will not know everything you need to know for the exam. If you start the night before, you will only have time to review a few major points. You might as well review them well and not spend any time stewing over what you are missing. If the instructor asks about the material you have not studied, you are simply out of luck. Next time, start studying earlier.

EXERCISE 6.2

When will you take your next exam or quiz? In your journal, design a study plan for that specific exam or quiz utilizing what you have learned about your memory. Write down what you will do, in what order, on what days. Now do it.

Summary

At the beginning of this chapter I mentioned students who would say "I really knew this stuff when I studied it; I just couldn't remember it on the day of the exam." By now it should be clear to you that they never understood the material well enough. There's a big difference between understanding a lecture or a page in your book and being able to recall it for a test. To do well in school, it is not enough to understand what you read or hear; you must be able to recall the information.

Recalling information means transferring it from long-term memory to short-term memory. In order to do that, it must first be stored in long-term memory. That doesn't happen automatically. You must pay attention, you must refresh your memory through repetition, and you must invest each item with meaning. Divide the material into chunks, review it often, and employ whatever mnemonic devices you find handy. You'll never have to complain that you really knew the material until you had to take the test.

II

How to Succeed in Specific Courses

In Part I you learned to create your own definition of success, how to manage your time, how to attack your coursework, how to learn outside of class, how to learn collaboratively, and how to use your memory. You are now equipped to succeed in college. Part II will show you some of the specific techniques you can use to put those principles to work. Chapter 7 will teach you how to learn from your lecture classes: how to listen, how to take notes effectively, and how to use your notes as effective tools for study. Chapter 8 will show you how to get the most out of reading your textbooks and will demonstrate some reading methods. Chapter 9 will help you see the value of learning from experience in laboratory courses, field experiences, and internships. Chapter 10 will teach you how to learn effectively in the courses and activities that require practice, such as mathematics, foreign language courses, and athletics.

7

Learning Through Lectures

➤ **M**ost of the courses you take in college will include lectures. You've been hearing lectures in classrooms at least since junior high school, so by now you should be used to them. Someone who is older than you, who probably knows more than you do (at least about the subject of the course), and who has more authority and power than you stands at the front of the classroom and tells you the truth for 50 minutes.

Lectures, by their very nature, tend to be boring. You are not actively involved in what's going on, and you have little control over what will happen next. Consequently, unless you are fascinated by the subject, your attention tends to wander. Some lecturers are good at keeping your attention; some are not. Even when lectures are boring, getting something out of them is crucial to succeeding in college. If you don't understand them or remember what was said, you will be in serious trouble on the exam.

This chapter will show you some of the techniques you can use to get the most out of your lectures. You will learn how to listen to lectures; how to take notes, study from them, and remember what they say; and how to supplement the lectures with material from other sources. Along the way you will learn how to make lecture courses more interesting.

How to Listen

You have been listening, and learning from what you heard, since before you were born. By now you are probably pretty

93

good at it. You understand everything your friends say, and you can respond appropriately; you can follow what the folks on TV or in a movie are saying; you can converse with your professors. Nonetheless, chances are good that you have difficulty paying close attention to many of your lectures. Why is that?

Listening is an active process. Think about a situation in which you listen the best: an intense conversation with a friend. You let your friend know that you are listening through attentive facial expressions and hand gestures; occasionally you encourage her by saying "yes" or "uh-huh"; sometimes you break in with a prompting question or reinforcing remark. In short, you are actively involved in those conversations.

Now think about what happens in a lecture. You sit, the lecturer stands. You listen, the lecturer talks. You are one of a crowd of 20, or 100, or 800; the lecturer is on his own. In most lectures, there is no possibility of a conversation. If you were to respond as you do with your friend—appropriate facial expressions and gestures, prompting questions, "uh-huh"—the lecturer would throw you out of class. You are not actively involved in what is going on. You are a passive recipient, not an active participant. Consequently you do not listen very well.

Psychologists have discovered that at any given moment in a lecture, only 20 percent of the students are actually paying attention.* And even those who are paying attention will retain only a fraction of what they hear. At the end of the lecture, students who were listening closely will remember about half of what they heard. The next day they will remember only 35 percent; within 2 months their retention is below 25 percent. So even when you pay close attention to a lecture, you simply cannot retain everything you hear. That makes listening closely crucial; if you do not listen well, you'll remember next to nothing. And if you remember next to nothing, you'll fare poorly on the test.

Listening successfully consists of four elements: hearing the lecture, paying attention to it, understanding what it means, and remembering it.

----

*Of the remainder, 20 percent (both men and women) are pursuing an erotic thought, 20 percent are reminiscing about something, and 40 percent are daydreaming, worrying, or anticipating lunch. (These statistics come from a paper given at a conference of the American Psychological Association, as summarized by R. Adler, L. Rosenfeld, and N. Towne, *Interplay: The Process of Interpersonal Communication*, 4th ed., NY, Holt, Rinehart & Winston, 1989, page 182.)

HEAR

In order to listen successfully, you must first hear what the lecturer is saying. Normally that's not a problem. Most lecture halls are acoustically adequate, and most students have normal hearing. However, if hearing the lecture is a problem for you, do something about it. Sit closer to the speaker or have your hearing checked. If the noisy students sitting around you are an obstacle to your hearing, make them shut up. If they won't, complain. Remember, you are paying for this lecture; you deserve to hear it.

ATTEND

Second, you must attend to what the lecturer is saying. Paying attention takes an act of will. You must decide that you are going to pay attention; you cannot wait to be motivated by the lecturer. Most college lecturers are at best adequate speakers. Only a few are the dynamic, exciting sorts of lecturers who can grab and hold your attention. Unfortunately, you have to take tests on the material from the most boring as well as the most exciting lectures you hear.

The best aid to paying attention is taking notes. It's hard to take notes without paying attention; the act of writing is one way to become actively involved. Even if you throw your notes away at the end of the lecture, taking them is worthwhile. The life cycle of the gypsy moth, for instance, may not grab you. You may be bored stiff by the principle of the golden mean or tectonic plate theory or standard deviations. But if you are trying to take accurate notes, you have to follow along just to get it all down.

UNDERSTAND

Third, you must understand what you are hearing. If the lecture is gibberish, you will never remember it. But if it makes sense to you, if the major points hang together in a coherent whole, you will remember large portions of it. Before the lecture starts, recall the major points of the last few lectures so that you have a context for today's material. And at the conclusion of the class, jot down the major point of the lecture—it will help you understand today's lecture tomorrow. If there are pieces of the lecture you don't understand, ask a question. If you don't understand it, there are at least a few others who are puzzled also.

REMEMBER

Finally, you must remember what you hear. If you don't remember it, what good is the lecture in the first place? To remember it—even to remember half of it, the best most people can do—you must place the material from the lecture into a larger whole. Draw some connections from today's lecture to previous lectures, to the supplementary reading you are doing for the course, to half-remembered concepts from high school, to your own experiences. Use some of the aids to memory described in Chapter 6, if that helps you. Turn lists of important concepts into acronyms, or associate important dates with your cousin's phone number. Jot those things down in your notes.

There are some tricks—in addition to heeding these four elements —that you can use to help you listen better.

BE CONSCIOUS OF YOUR GOALS

Why are you taking this course? What grade do you want to achieve? What grade do you need on the next test? Paying attention is always easier when you have some personal involvement in what is being said. If the lecture is squarely within your major field, you are probably already interested enough in the topic to maintain your attention. On the other hand, if the lecture is part of a class you are taking merely to meet a graduation requirement, you may have a harder time. Generating a feeling of personal involvement in the life cycle of the gypsy moth can be difficult if you are not a biology major. But you can always crank up strong feelings about your grades. Write your grade goals at the beginning of each day's lecture notes; that will help you concentrate.

FILL IN THE GAPS

One of the barriers to effective listening is the difference between the speed with which we think and the speed with which other people talk. We are capable of thinking at a rate of about 600 words per minute, but people talk at a rate of 100 to 140 words per minute. So we tend to fill in the gaps with our own thoughts. Sometimes our thoughts are more intriguing than what we are hearing, so we tune out the lecture in favor of an internal monologue. Consequently our attention wanders, and we cease listening.

You can't make your professors talk faster. But you can work at controlling your internal monologue so that it contributes to your understanding of the lecture instead of obstructing it. Instead of filling in the gaps left by his 100-words-per-minute lecture with reminiscences about last night's party or anticipations of lunch, fill them in with supplementary information about the course. Plug in a relevant fact from last week's reading assignment or an experience of your own that illustrates his point. Speculate on what might be the topic of tomorrow's lecture. Generate some possible quiz questions he might ask. Make up a question you can ask after class.

LISTEN CRITICALLY

Whenever the lecturer makes a major point, ask yourself "Is that true?" A good lecturer will have already given you the supporting evidence for that point, or will soon thereafter. Does that evidence convince you? If there is counterevidence, jot it down in your notes. Chances are your instructor will get to the counterevidence sooner or later. (If she doesn't, ask about it, either in class or during office hours. Even if you are off base, she'll be impressed that you were thinking about what she said.) Don't discount the points you don't agree with; you must remember this material for the test whether you agree with it or not. But listening critically to a lecture will help you remember it.

WRITE CONSTANTLY

If none of these tricks seems to work, here's one that will: Take notes constantly. Write down everything the lecturer says, even the tirades about the dean or the nostalgic reminiscences about his days as an undergraduate. Writing constantly is a way to involve yourself actively in what's going on. Your hand will tire, but it will soon recover. And your notes will be a fairly complete record of the class. Best of all, you will have paid attention.

The point of all of these tricks is to get you actively involved in listening to the lecture. The setting and the format of lectures conspire to keep you passive. But you don't learn very much when you are passive, so you must do whatever you can to counteract their effects. Being conscious of your goals, filling in the gaps with supplementary material, and listening critically will keep you actively involved in what's going on in the class. And being actively involved will help you listen to the lecture and retain what you hear.

Taking Notes

You have already learned that the best reason for taking notes is to help you pay attention. But there are other reasons as well. Your notes will help you prepare for quizzes and exams. Taking notes helps you keep track of what the lecturer is saying, so if you are puzzled 5 minutes from now you can look back through your notes and figure out the background. You can get a head start on some assignments in your notebook; when your instructor assigns a paper, for instance, you can brainstorm on possible topics in your notebook, sketch out a preliminary outline, and so on. But the primary reason for taking notes is to help you listen.

How should you do it? Well, there are lots of ways. But all of them share these basic principles.

USE WHATEVER METHOD WORKS

Always remember that the primary reason for taking notes in the first place is to help you attend to the lecture. Don't let your roommate's note-taking method, the outline method from sixth grade, or your mom's parting advice to write down only the most important stuff get in your way. On the other hand, don't ignore the other reasons for taking notes: gathering study material for the test, getting a head start on assignments, generating questions, and so on. Figure out which method works for you, and use it.

REVIEW YOUR NOTES
BEFORE THE NEXT LECTURE

Read over your notes the evening you take them, or while standing in the breakfast line the next morning, or while riding in the car pool to school, or just before the next meeting of the class. It doesn't take long to review your notes if you do it before the next class meeting because the material is still fresh in your mind. Five or 10 minutes should suffice. In those 5 minutes you will reinforce your already fading memories of the lecture, and that reinforcement will help you store it away for future use.

If you wait to review your notes until the night before the exam, each set of class notes will take much more than 5 minutes. You won't be able to figure out half of the references, some of the terms will be puzzling, and the arguments will have gaps. You might have to spend half an hour reconstructing a set of notes. Better to invest 5 minutes the day after class.

TAKE NOTES
ON YOUR NOTES

Whenever you review your notes, use your pencil. Fill in the gaps in the arguments, write in definitions of puzzling terms, and make the references clear. Add whatever supplementary information you can from your reading or your own experience. Your notes-on-notes will be much more complete and therefore much more helpful when you study for the exam. In addition, writing while you review helps keep you actively engaged. When you are using your pencil it is difficult for you to fall into that glazed-eye state we have all experienced from time to time, where the eyes drift down the page but no information gets through to the brain.

Using a loose-leaf notebook for your notes will allow you to add extra pages whenever and wherever you need them, so you can write as many notes-on-notes as you like. But you can still use this trick even if you use a spiral-bound notebook. Make sure you write on only one side of the page; that way you can write your notes-on-notes on the facing page. Whichever kind of notebook you use, start at the top of a clean page for every lecture. Write the date and the course name. And leave lots of white space. Skip lines frequently, set wide margins, and leave an inch or two on the top and bottom. You'll spend a few more dollars on paper that way, but paper is cheaper than tuition.

PAY PARTICULAR ATTENTION
TO THE BEGINNING AND END

Most professors begin their lectures by summarizing the previous lecture and then introducing the topic for the day. The summary of the previous lecture will help give you a framework for what you are about to hear. The introduction to today's lecture will give you an idea of the main points of the lecture to come. Knowing what those main points are in advance will help you organize your notes as you write them. When you hear a new main point, make a new paragraph or a new heading, or underline it.

Don't leave it at that; you need more than main points. Record the explanation of each point and some illustrative examples. The explanation will help you understand it later, and the examples will be invaluable on the exam. Professors are always impressed when you use the same examples they did in their lectures. They take it as a sign that you are as smart as they are.

At the end of the lecture, most professors summarize what they have said. Pay close attention. Take that opportunity to go back over your notes to make sure you got the main points. If you didn't, race to the front of the room to ask about whatever it was you missed. You will never have a better opportunity to fill in that gap, and the lecturer will be pleased at your diligence.

PAY ATTENTION
TO SIGNAL WORDS

"Therefore" or "so" means there is a conclusion coming. It may be a main point, it may be a minor point, but in either case it is a conclusion and is probably worth noting. Make sure you also note the premises that support the conclusion. Premises are signaled by words like "since," "because," and "for these reasons." These words and phrases introduce supporting evidence for the conclusion.

"Furthermore" and "in addition" signal more support for the same point. "For example" lets you know that an example illustrating a general point is on the way. Note it; examples not only help you understand generalizations, they also show the instructor that you understand them when you write them into an answer to an essay question.

"In other words," "in essence," and "briefly" introduce a simplified explanation of whatever has just been said. Usually these simplified explanations are worth noting, because they can help you understand later and may also serve as a good explanation to use on short-answer tests. "Most importantly," "above all," and "remember that" are emphasis words. They let you know that what is to follow is important; you had better write it down, and you had better remember it.

Sometimes a professor will follow her conclusion by saying "on the other hand" or "conversely"; those words signal a contrast to the conclusion she has just drawn. (Don't be led into the trap of thinking that she has just refuted her previous conclusion. She probably has not; she just wants you to know that there are other points of view on this point. Doubtless she will go on to destroy that conflicting point of view.)

All lecturers use a set of nonverbal signals in addition to signal words. Some will raise their voices when they come to the most important points, some will repeat them, some will count them off on their fingers, and some will write them on the board. You will catch on to those systems of signals within the first week of class. Use your knowledge. When a board-writer writes something on the board, duplicate it in your notes along with the explanations that he provides verbally. When you hear a repeater saying the same phrase twice, make sure it appears prominently in your notes. When a voice-raiser increases the volume, listen up.

USE SOME SORT OF SHORTHAND
IN YOUR NOTES

You can't write as fast as your lecturers speak; therefore you will have to compress their lectures as you take your notes. Do *not* use the kind of shorthand you learned in secretarial science class in high school, in which symbols take the place of words. That sort of shorthand works against efficient note taking because the words used in most lectures don't lend themselves to the standard symbols. Besides, using some formal system of shorthand will take some concentration, and you should be concentrating on the lecture. Develop your own system of shorthand a little at a time as you take your notes. That way it will be natural to you and will not require any thought.

Use as many standard abbreviations as you know: "cf" for "compare," "eg" for "for example," "Engl" for "England," and "NYC" for "New York City." Don't bother putting periods after them. Abbreviate the words you write most often: "tf" for "therefore," "subj" for "subject," "conc" for "concentration," and so on. Make up your own abbreviations as you go along. For instance, leave the vowels out of long words, as if you were writing an ad for the classified advertisement section of the newspaper. Or leave the endings off of academic words:

"econ" and "phil" for "economics" and "philosophy." But be sure to spell out the word or phrase the first time you use it so you won't forget what the abbreviation means.

Just as you can leave vowels out of long words, you can leave words out of sentences. Short words such as articles ("a," "the," "an") and connectives ("and," "or," "but") can frequently be left out of sentences without changing the meaning. When a lecturer says "There are three basic causes of crime: poverty, moral decadence, and greed," your notes should say something like "3 causes crime—poverty, moral decadence, greed." Don't worry about capitalization, punctuation, spelling, or any of the standard conventions of writing. Like your journal, your notes are meant to communicate only with you; if you can understand them next time you read them, they're good enough.

DON'T TRANSCRIBE

Many students come to college thinking that they are going to scribble notes in class, and then type or copy them later so they are legible and usable. Don't do it. Transcribing notes takes a lot of time; you'll be better off using that time for study or recreation. So don't scribble your notes; write them legibly enough to read later. (That doesn't mean following the Palmer method of penmanship, or dotting all of your *i*'s, or using proper punctuation. None of that matters. But you must be able to decipher your notes.) If you review them before the next class meeting, you can clean them up well enough to read before the exam.

Don't tape-record your lectures. For one thing, your professors may object. Their lectures are their intellectual property, and it is against the law for you to record them without permission. More importantly, recording lectures won't give you any usable notes; all it will give you is a duplicate lecture. To make use of it, you'll have to listen to it again and take notes on it. But you can do that in class and save the extra hours you would spend listening to the recording.

If you follow these basic principles, your notes will work for you no matter what method of note taking you use.

Note-Taking Techniques

Dozens of methods of taking notes have been invented over the years. I'll show you several. Use whichever method works the best for you.

Feel free to adapt any or all of these methods in any ways you choose. The goal is to help you concentrate and give you some study material for later review; use whatever helps you reach that goal.

If you have taken notes regularly in recent years (in high school classes, or for the minutes of meetings, or to keep a record of important conversations at work), you probably are pretty good at it by now. And the method you have developed probably works well for you. Still, you may learn some new tricks by trying one of these methods. If you have never taken notes, you may have no idea how to go about it. Try each of these methods in turn to see which one works best for you. You will probably wind up with a method of taking notes that combines features of each of these methods.

THE WRITE-IT-ALL-DOWN METHOD

Many first-time notetakers try to write down everything the instructor says. That's not a bad approach. It will help you concentrate on the lecture and will give you a fairly complete record of the class. There are some disadvantages. You will emerge from class with a cramped hand and pages of scribbles. Your hand will swiftly recover, but your scribbles will need further work before you can make use of them.

Write-it-all-down notetakers *must* develop some sort of shorthand. Use all of the tricks outlined earlier and develop more on your own. Try to condense the lecturer's long, rambling sentences into short, concise phrases. Try to leave nonessential words out of sentences and nonessential letters out of words. But don't stop your note taking to abbreviate or break your concentration; when in doubt, write it down.

Try to organize your notes as you go along. At least break the stream of words into paragraphs. Every time the lecturer makes a new point, start a new paragraph. Leave a blank line between paragraphs; later on you can use those blank lines to add headings for the most important paragraphs. As she explains her point with examples, explanations, and so on, add sentences to your paragraph. New point; new paragraph. It's sometimes hard to tell the difference between an illustration of an old point and the introduction of a new one. Do the best you can, and if it turns out that you buried a main point in the middle of a paragraph, go back and underline or circle it.

Note that you are already editing what your instructor says. You are leaving out some words she speaks and some of the letters of the words you include. You are organizing what you hear as you go along.

In other words, even if you are trying to write down everything she says, you are really interpreting her words and reproducing your own version of them. The more of that interpretation you do, the more helpful your notes will be because the more you interpret the lecture, the more you think about it. And the more you think about it, the more meaning you will invest in it and the more you will remember. Notes you take while you are actively thinking will reflect that thinking, and they will therefore help you remember better when you prepare for the exam.

Figure 7.1 is a page of notes taken early in a course called Introduction to Ecological Systems. The notetaker is trying to write down everything the instructor says and is doing a fairly good job. He has already developed some shorthand. He abbreviates "introduction," "agriculture," "civilization," and "hunter–gatherers"; he writes "ie" instead of "that is," and "w/" instead of "with"; he leaves out inessential words and phrases. He has also invented some symbols of his own. An arrow signals a result or a consequence. Three dots means "thus," signaling a conclusion or a summary.

Writing down everything you hear is a perfectly acceptable method of taking notes. It works especially well in classes like philosophy, literature, or history, in which lectures usually take the form of narratives. It works less well in science classes, in which lectures are explanations frequently accompanied by demonstrations or models. Nonetheless, many students have succeeded in college through writing down everything they hear in lectures.

THE OUTLINE METHOD

You were probably taught the outline method back in seventh or eighth grade, when your English teachers started warning you how hard college was going to be. "You'll never make it through college dawdling through class the way you have today; I'm going to show you how to take notes so you'll be ready for the ordeal." And so they taught you to use a loose-leaf notebook, lined paper with a vertical red line an inch from the left edge, and a sharp pencil. Put main points flush against the red line on the left, identified with roman numerals. Indent subordinate points under them, and identify them with capital letters. Indent points that are more subordinate even farther, identified with numbers. And so on. "But remember, boys and girls, you must never have a single subordinate point in your outline. If you have an A, you must have at least a B; if you have a 1, you must have a 2."

Figure 7.1 *Sample notes: write-it-all-down method*

> ### Intro to Ecological Systems
> #### 9/17 History of Agriculture
>
> Original societies hunter-gatherers—
> ie food, etc, from plants + animals they
> found, <u>not grew.</u> No civ possible — all time
> spent hunting/gathering. Civ only possible
> w/dev't of ag.
>
> 5 major crops in world today, each led
> to a diff civ — wheat, corn, potatoes, rice,
> soybeans.
>
> <u>Wheat</u> 10K ± years ago h-g civ in Tigris-
> Euphrates Valley discovered wild grasses
> (have edible seeds) can be grown — soon —
> barley + wheat. W/steady food supply, no
> need to wander — can build towns near
> fields. Can spend time thinking, dreaming,
> learning (→ education systems, leisure
> activities, arts). Can spend time trading
> surplus goods (→ money, counting systems,
> banks, commerce + trade). ∴ wheat basis
> for Western civ.

This method is wonderful for taking notes—if the lecturer speaks in outline form. Some do. I have even known lecturers who say "Roman numeral I: . . . A: . . . B: . . ."—but most do not. Most lecturers have a few main points, a lot of explanatory material, and a few jokes. It comes out in a jumbled stream, not in an outline. Of course that stream can be translated into an outline, with the main points bearing roman numerals, the explanatory material divided up into subordinate points, and the jokes discarded. But to do so would take far more effort than the product would be worth. You're better off using a much simpler method of outlining. And if you leave a hanging A or 1, don't worry about it.

Figure 7.2 shows notes taken in modified outline form from the same lecture on the history of agriculture. The lecturer began by discussing hunter–gatherer societies; that became item I. She then turned to the development of modern civilizations; that became item II. When he reviewed his notes that evening, the notetaker realized that her remarks on hunter–gatherer societies were merely a prelude to the main topic—how agriculture creates civilizations—and so he went back and starred item II with a downward-pointing arrow in the margin as a signal that this is crucial material. At the same time he added a few notes-on-notes.

Some courses are more amenable to the outline method of note taking than others. Zoology lectures in which the instructor is particularly well organized, for instance, will sometimes divide themselves into discrete units devoted to genus, species, and so on. Outlines are good for duplicating that structure. Other courses are not amenable to outlines. A rambling lecture on Elizabethan life for a course on Shakespeare would be very difficult to record in outline form. But if you are comfortable with the outline method and if it works for you, use it.

Many students wind up using some combination of the write-it-all-down and the outline methods. They find that writing it all down is a terrible chore and taxes their concentration. But outlines are too rigid to follow. So they develop a combined style in which main ideas are identified by numbers and letters showing whatever organization clearly emerges from the lecture, but the professor's explanations and subordinate points are recorded in sentences and paragraphs.

THE CORNELL METHOD

Walter Pauk,* who has studied and written more about study skills than anyone else, first developed the Cornell system of taking notes for his students at Cornell University about 40 years ago. It has spread

---

*See Walter Pauk, *How to Study in College*, 4th ed., Boston, MA, Houghton Mifflin, 1989, for an extremely complete treatise on study skills. His description of the Cornell method is on pages 144–153.

Figure 7.2 *Sample notes: outline method*

Intro to Ecological Systems
9\17   History of Agriculture

I Hunter/gatherer societies
   A. gathered or hunted all food + supplies
   B. therefore no civilization possible —
      no time, constantly wandering

✳ II Civilized societies
   A. formed only after development of
      agriculture
   B. different crop → different civ.
   C. 5 major crops (wheat, corn, potatoes,
      rice, soybeans)
      1. <u>Wheat</u>
         a. 1st cultivated 10,000 years
           ago — Tigris-Euphrates Valley
           (cradle of civ means Western
           civ)

ag produces civilization!

         b. came — we think! — from
           wild grasses, became barley,
           wheat
         c. wheat stores well, travels
           well, so frees up time —
         d. result: expanded learning,
           arts, trade, money
      2. <u>Corn</u>

widely since then. If anyone other than your seventh-grade English teacher has taught you a note-taking system, chances are it is the Cornell method.

To use the Cornell method you must modify the sheets of paper you take notes on. Use standard, lined, 8½-by-11-inch notebook paper, either loose-leaf or spiral-bound. Draw a horizontal line across the page 2 inches from the bottom. Now draw a vertical line 2½ inches from the left edge of the page from the very top to the horizontal line you just drew. Your finished product should be a lined sheet of paper with three spaces to write in: a 2-inch space stretching across the bottom of the page, a 2½-inch space along the left margin, and a 6-by-9-inch space filling most of the sheet.

When you take notes, record what happens in class in the 6-by-9-inch space. Use your own shorthand, write legibly enough to read it later, and include as much of the lecture as you can. Immediately after class, go over your notes to fill in any blanks you may have left.

Before your next class meeting, go over your notes. For each fact or idea, extract a key word or phrase. Write it in the space along the left margin next to the fact or idea it summarizes. When you review, cover the body of your notes with a piece of blank paper. Read each of the key words or phrases aloud, and then recite—*aloud*—the fact or idea it summarizes. Check your memory against your notes. If you remembered poorly, do it again.

Alternatively, formulate a question based on each fact or idea in your notes, and write the question in the left-hand space. Reviewing, then, is simply a matter of asking yourself the questions in the left-hand column and reciting the answers.

Reciting this material aloud will help cement each bit of information in your memory. You have already read about the value of actively engaging yourself in your learning. Reciting is one way to engage yourself. Psychologists and elementary school teachers have known for years that one of the best ways to learn something is to say it aloud. Reciting helps you internalize what's in your notes and make it your own. Don't worry about making a fool of yourself in front of your roommate and friends. If you study within earshot of anyone, recite very quietly; the technique is just as effective at a whisper as at a shout.

After you have used the left-hand column to review, write a summary of the entire page of notes in the space you have left at the bottom of the page. On the bottom of the last page for that particular lecture, summarize the entire lecture. Writing this summary has two benefits: Doing it will help you pull the lecture's information together in your mind, and the summaries you write will serve you well when you study for the exam.

Figure 7.3 *Sample notes: Cornell method*

	Intro to Eco Systems
	History of Agriculture
Hunter-gatherers nomads	Hunter-gatherers (found all food + supplies in surroundings, grew nothing) — nomadic. Predecessor of all civilizations. Civ only possible w/ agriculture. Today, 5 major crops on earth— wheat, corn, potatoes, rice, soybeans. Each one started a civ.
Ag → civ	
Wheat 10K years ago Tigris-Euphrates	Wheat — anthro + history think started 10K years ago in Tigris-Euphrates Valley, Near East. Probably started planting wild grasses, turned into barley + wheat. Wheat stores well, travels, rises (bread), good protein. Made possible leisure time, mathematics (to count, trade, etc), arts, keeping of animals, armies (can carry food), trade (surplus wheat for goods), beer.
stores, travels, protein, rises	
Leisure activities, math, arts, trade, war	
	Western civ started w/ dev't of wheat.

The Cornell method is depicted in Figure 7.3. The largest space on the page is filled with notes taken as the lecturer spoke. Afterward, the notetaker wrote a few key words or phrases in the left margin and used them to review. Finally, he wrote a summary of the page in the space at the bottom of the page.

Note that these sets of notes taken on the same lecture differ somewhat in content as well as in format. Different students record lectures differently. One student may already know a lot about hunter–gatherer societies. She need only write a word or two about them. Another may not be familiar with the concept at all, and will therefore write more. Still, all three of these students captured the major points of the lecture. And they all paid attention throughout, so their note taking was successful.

You can use the Cornell method with the write-it-all-down method, with the outline method, or with whatever method you develop on your own. Divide up your paper; take notes using your favorite method in the biggest space, and then write key words and phrases or questions in the left-hand space. Recite. Write summaries in the bottom space, and use those summaries to review.

Actually, you can use the essential elements of the Cornell method without dividing up your paper. If you write on only one side of the pages in your notebook, you can write your key words, phrases, questions, and summaries on the facing page. In effect, you are taking notes on your notes—one of the basic principles of effective note taking. If you review before the next class, you are reinforcing your memory of the important ideas in the lecture before it is superceded by the next lecture. And if you recite, summarize, and review, you are actively engaging yourself in the material.

EXERCISE 7.2

Use the Cornell method of taking notes in two different courses. Divide your page beforehand, take your notes, write in your key words, recite, summarize, review. Did using this system help you get more out of those lectures? In your journal, write for 10 minutes on the best method of taking notes for you.

Adding Supplementary Material

No matter which system of note taking you use, your notes form the basis for your studying. Consequently, anything that is important to the course should appear somewhere in your notes. For a chemistry class, you might attach your lab notes to your notes on the lecture explaining the lab. For a philosophy class in which the lectures explain and comment upon readings, you might integrate your lecture notes and your reading notes (the next chapter will tell you how). For a biology class that depends heavily upon observations in the field, you might add field descriptions to your lecture notes. For all of these courses, combining your lecture notes with whatever supplementary material is available will place all of the material you need to study for the exam in one place.

You can most easily integrate supplementary material into your lecture notes by using a loose-leaf notebook for each course. With a loose-leaf, you can insert pages wherever you like. Put your lab notes next to the lecture notes that explain the main points of the lab. Put your reading notes next to the lecture notes that explain and comment upon that reading. Put your field descriptions next to the lecture that described and explained what you saw.

Remember to start each entry—lecture, lab, reading, field trip— on a clean sheet and to write on only one side. That way you never have to worry about ripping pages in two because they contain pieces of two lectures. At the end of the quarter or semester, you can store your notes for each course in file folders (don't throw them out; you may have to refer to them someday for another course), and reuse the loose-leaf binders for your new courses.

Even if you don't use loose-leaf binders, you can still add supplementary material to your notes. If you use a spiral-bound notebook for each course, for instance, you can add brief notes on the blank side of the page. (You only wrote your lecture notes on one side, remember?) You may get a little cramped because you will also use that space for your notes-on-notes. But if you leave enough white space to start with and you write small, you can make it work. At least you can make it work better than not adding supplementary material at all.

Don't ignore your own experiences as you are adding supplementary material. Keep in mind that the academic subjects that seem so abstract and arcane to you all stem from the curiosity of an individual person just like you. People began studying physics because they wanted to know the rules by which physical objects behave. The rules they discovered—the abstract formulas you work so hard to learn and understand in physics class—are nothing more than numerical summaries of their experience with physical objects. You have that experience, too. You witness objects falling downwards, you see light bending through lenses, you use electricity all the time. Your experiences are relevant to physics. The same is true for biology, political science, business, and every other academic subject.

Whenever you hear a lecture, read a text, or do a laboratory experiment, you should try to relate what you are hearing or reading or seeing to your own experience. Bring the abstract generalizations you deal with in class down to earth by translating them into something you have direct experience with. You will understand them better, and you will remember them longer. Jot those experiences down in your notes. When your philosophy instructor is describing utilitarian ethical theories ("the greatest good for the greatest number"), remember the method the Circle K club in high school used to decide how to spend the proceeds of the car wash. Write "car wash" in the margin of your notes. When your biology instructor describes the regenerative properties of certain sorts of tissue, remember watching your son's pet lizard regenerate its own tail after being squished under the rocking chair, and write "Freddie the lizard" in your notes.

Summary

This chapter has taught you that the most important reason to take notes is to help you concentrate on what goes on in class. That's not the only reason, however; your notes will also serve you well in studying for the exam, in generating ideas for papers and projects, and in figuring out difficult topics.

The basic principles of good note taking are: Use your notes to help you pay attention; review your notes before the next lecture; take notes on your notes; pay particular attention to the beginning and end of the lecture; pay attention to signal words; use some sort of shorthand; don't transcribe or copy your notes. As long as you follow these principles, your notes will help you understand the course material and do well on the exam.

There are many methods of taking notes. This chapter described three: the write-it-all-down method, the outline method, and the Cornell method. They are not mutually exclusive. You may like the overall structure of the Cornell method and follow its page layout. You may use the write-it-all-down method for your straight lecture classes and the outline method for your science and math classes. Wonderful. Use whatever method helps you reach your academic goals.

What goes on in class is the heart of most courses. (There are exceptions. As a junior or senior, you may take an independent study course, in which you read a lot and write a paper on the basis of your reading. Or you may take a seminar, in which the bulk of your learning comes from the papers you write.) So your class notes are important. Make sure that they reflect what happened in class and that they include whatever supplementary material is important: readings, experiments, field trips. And bring them to a personal level by adding illustrative examples from your own experience.

8

Learning Through Reading

Most of your courses will require at least some reading. And some of your courses will use textbooks as the primary delivery system, so most of the information you are responsible for on the exam comes from your reading. No problem, right? You've been reading since first grade. Wrong. The way you learned to read in elementary school—"start at the beginning, read and understand every word, don't jump ahead, finish every book you start"—will not help you much in reading your texts. If you read your history or chemistry or speech textbooks that way, you'll never get all of your work done. This chapter will show you how to read your texts efficiently with maximum results in minimal time.

How to Read

You already know how to read, or you wouldn't be reading this book. But you probably don't know how to read a text. Reading a text is very different from reading a newspaper, magazine, or novel. The biggest difference is that you read newspapers, magazines, and novels for your own purposes: to entertain yourself, to satisfy your curiosity, to pass the time. If you are not entertained, if your curiosity is not satisfied, if the time passes too slowly, you stop reading. But you read texts to satisfy the purposes of someone else—your professor. If you are not entertained or your curiosity is not satisfied or the time passes slowly, you can't dump your text the way you can dump a newpaper. You must read it anyway. And so you sigh, shake your head, and grind it out.

Many students are bored by the reading they must do for their courses, at least some of the time. Some students are bored by their course reading all of the time. Nonetheless, it has to be done. If you don't do your reading, the lectures will mean little to you. Most lecturers assume that students have completed the assigned reading before they come to class, and they design their lectures to fill in the gaps. If you don't do your reading, you're going to miss the significance of a large portion of the lecture. Furthermore, if you don't read you are exiling yourself from the long and interesting tradition of learning in Western civilization. Worst of all, if you don't do your reading you are likely to be in big trouble on the exam.

So how should you read? First, forget much of what you learned in elementary school. You *don't* have to start at the beginning, you *don't* have to read and understand every word, you *can* jump ahead, you *don't* have to finish every book you start. You had to do those things when you were 8 so that you could develop your linguistic skills. But your linguistic skills are mostly developed now, so forget those rules. Instead, follow these basic principles.

READ ACTIVELY

You have already learned the value of being actively engaged in what you are doing. The last chapter taught you how to be actively engaged in listening to a lecture. You should also be actively involved in reading your assignments. It's not easy; reading is by nature a passive activity. You sit still, the only part of your body that moves is your eyes, and the purpose is to receive information from an external source—the book. But you can increase your level of activity so you do become actively engaged in what's going on.

Always read with a pencil in your hand, and use it. It doesn't matter much what you use it for—underline key phrases, write in the margin, or take notes in your loose-leaf—as long as you are using it while you read. Just as taking notes in class helps you attend to the lecture, using your pencil while you read helps you attend to what you are reading.

Some students like to use light-colored magic markers to block out significant pieces of text. That's fine, if it works for you. I find that method slow, and the squeaks the marker makes are distracting to me and everyone else around me. Besides, it's hard to write in the margins with a marker. Other students use a pen or pencil, underlining and circling key words or phrases, blocking significant chunks of text with vertical lines next to them, and writing questions and brief summaries in the margins. That's fine too, if it works. The important thing is to be using your pencil, pen, or marker while you read. I once knew a wonderful high school teacher who taught all her students that they couldn't think without a pencil in their hands. They believed her and did very well.

Don't let your pencil take control of you. Sometimes students worry so much about what they should be marking or writing in the margins that they cannot concentrate on what they are reading. Remember that the primary reason for using your pencil is to help you concentrate; don't let the pencil block your concentration. Some students find that their pencils help them concentrate the best if they read a paragraph or section first, and then go back and mark it up.

KNOW WHAT THE READING IS ABOUT BEFORE YOU START

Sounds weird, doesn't it? How can you know what a book or passage is about before you read it? There are several ways. The title tells you something, and all of the subtitles and headings throughout the text will tell you more. So leaf through the pages you will read before you actually start reading them to survey the titles and headings. If there are illustrations—photographs, charts, graphs, diagrams—look at them and read the captions. Most authors use illustrations to illuminate their main points, so surveying them will give you a quick notion of what's most important. Some books, like this one, introduce each chapter with a few paragraphs that tell you what's coming and conclude with a brief summary. Read them. Some books close each section with a few study questions. Look closely at them; they will tell you which points are most significant. Some instructors will give you a hint of what the reading is about when they make their assignments. Pay attention, and write what they say in your notes.

Knowing what your reading is about before you read it will save you a great deal of time. That sounds weird too, right? Doing these prereading exercises (that's what reading teachers call them) adds yet another chore to an already long list of things you have to do. But think of it this way. If you begin your reading cold, with no notion of what is to come, you have to figure it all out as you go along. And that takes a lot of time, especially with a complicated text. But if you know beforehand what the author is trying to prove, you have a head start. Your actual reading will go much faster, simply because you already have some idea of what's important and what you can ignore.

Knowing where the author is headed also will help keep you actively engaged in your reading. Now you have a stake in what's going on, and you can get caught up in the argument. "How can he possibly draw that conclusion?" you can ask yourself. "What's the relevance of that strange picture three pages ahead?" "Has he considered last year's developments in this field?" By reading, you find out.

ADJUST YOUR STYLE OF READING TO THE TASK AT HAND

There are two factors to consider: your own goals for the course and the nature of the reading assignment. If your goal for a modern American literature course is to get an A, then you may have to read all of the assignments with some care. You will need to know the story lines of all of the novels and stories you read, as well as the literary devices their authors employ. You will need to know something about those authors and how they fit into the history of American literature. You will need to be able to compare and contrast different works to answer essay questions on the exam, and you will need to analyze a few works for the papers you will write. In order to do all of that you must read diligently, actively, and closely.

If, on the other hand, your goal is to get a C, you can do a great deal less. You will still need to know the basic plots of all the novels and short stories you read as well as something about their authors, but you can probably write C answers to essay questions without knowing much about literary devices or the history of American literature. You will have to read one or two works closely to write your papers, but you can probably skim everything else. In short, your goals for a particular course will help determine how much you put into the reading for that course.

Some of your reading assignments demand closer attention than others. In a history course devoted to U.S. history since World War II, for example, you might have one primary text and three supplementary texts. The primary text is a survey of the period; it gives you the bulk of the information you need. The supplementary texts are novels set in particular time periods; they give you the flavor of those times. You should read the primary text regularly and closely, with pencil in hand, looking for facts, dates, trends, important personages, explanations of events, and so on. Read the novels more casually; look for examples that will bring to life the history you are learning through your primary text.

AFTER YOU READ, WRITE

Spend 5 or 10 minutes briefly summarizing and reacting to the reading in your notebook or journal. Don't try to duplicate what you've just read, and don't worry a great deal about the accuracy of what you write. Jot down the main idea and one or two subordinate points, and add your reaction: Did you like it? Is the author correct? Is the main idea well supported? Is there any counterevidence not mentioned by the author? Is it relevant to any of your other coursework? The point is to force yourself to think about what you have just read. When you write, you think; what you think about, you remember.

Review what you have written before the lecture devoted to that bit of reading. Your memory of what the author had to say will be refreshed, and you will be prepared for any class discussion about the reading. Reviewing before class will also help you integrate the information you received from your reading with the information you hear in the lecture—at least in your head.

ALWAYS LOOK FOR
THE ARGUMENT

Most academic writing is argumentative; it tries to prove something. I suggested earlier that you look through your text before you read it to find out what major point the author is making. That's the conclusion of the argument. When you read you should look for the premises leading the author to that conclusion and the trail of reasoning that gets him there. If you understand the argument, you understand the reading. And you will probably be able to remember it. Grasping premises, reasoning, and conclusion helps you see them all hang together in a memorable fashion.

EXERCISE 8.1

Describe in your journal the system of reading you have been using. Is it good enough? Which of the basic principles described in this chapter does your method incorporate?

Reading Techniques

Psychologists and educators have created many different methods of reading that employ the principles described in the previous section. Several of them are described in the following sections. Try them out. You may find that one of them is exactly right for you, or that pieces of two of them are helpful, or that none of them exactly fits your own learning style. Use whatever works.

SQ3R

This is the old standby among reading techniques. It stands for *survey, question, read, recite, review.* SQ3R was invented during World War II by Francis Robinson, a psychologist, to help military personnel undergoing accelerated university courses. It worked well. It still works well, especially for texts you must understand thoroughly and remember completely.

Follow these steps.

Survey Before you start reading, leaf through the reading assignment looking for the main ideas. Read headings and subheadings, captions, and so on. Take no more than a minute or two to survey a chapter, 5 or 10 minutes for an entire book.

Question Generate a question from the first section of your text. The quickest way is to turn the heading of the section into a question. Your psychology text might have "Dyslexia" as a subheading, for instance; an appropriate question is, what is dyslexia? If your text has no headings, make up a question based on your initial survey. If all else fails, ask yourself, what is this section about? Generating questions will stimulate your curiosity and get you actively involved in the text. When you are actively involved, you concentrate and remember better.

Read Read the first section to answer the question you generated. Having the question before you will give you a goal to work toward.

Recite Look away from the book and recite the answer to your question. Use your own words. Once you have recited, write down the question and answer in the margin or in your notebook. Now repeat the question, read, and recite steps for each section of your reading assignment.

Figure 8.1 shows how your textbook should look after going through this process. The text shown is a popular text for informal logic courses by Howard Kahane.*

Review   When you have completed the assignment, look over your notes to get an overview of the entire reading. Identify the main idea and the subordinate ideas that support it. Jot down a few examples that illustrate those ideas. Finally, write a one paragraph summary.

Note that the SQ3R method uses each of the basic principles listed in the previous section. You must become actively involved, you must preread, you must adjust your technique to the task at hand (you use SQ3R to read things closely), you must write after you read, and you must look for the argument (by looking for answers to questions).

3R

If you need not work through a reading assignment quite as thoroughly as SQ3R will force you to do, try the 3R method. 3R—*read, record*, and *recite*—works well if you need to know what a passage says, but not why it says it.

Read   Read a few paragraphs and then go back to the beginning. For each paragraph, ask yourself, "What do I need to know in this paragraph?" Reread until you can answer that question.

Record   Once you have answered that question, underline or block the word, phrase, or sentence that contains or identifies what you need to know. When you review, your eye will naturally go to what you have underlined. The underlined passage will remind you of what you decided was important in that paragraph. Read and record the entire assignment in this way.

Figure 8.2 shows the same page from Kahane after a student used the 3R method. Note that only the most important portions are blocked, and only key phrases (such as "deductively valid argument") or crucial signal words ("fundamental difference") are underlined. Examples of the two kinds of arguments discussed are noted in the margin.

Recite   Go over the entire reading assignment, reminding yourself of the important points in each paragraph. Finally, write a brief

---

*H. Kahane, *Logic and Contemporary Rhetoric*, 5th ed., Belmont, CA, Wadsworth, 1988. Reprinted by permission of the publisher.

Figure 8.1 *Textbook annotation: SQ3R method*

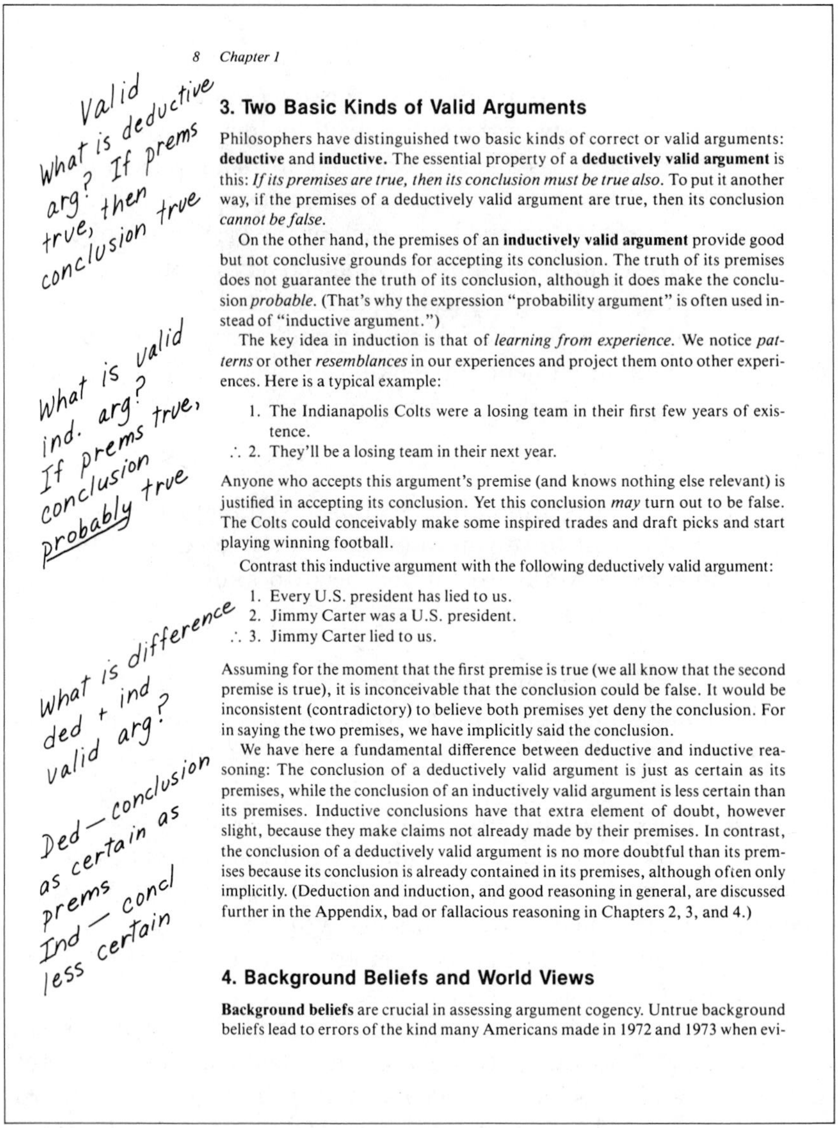

8 Chapter 1

3. Two Basic Kinds of Valid Arguments

Philosophers have distinguished two basic kinds of correct or valid arguments: **deductive** and **inductive.** The essential property of a **deductively valid argument** is this: *If its premises are true, then its conclusion must be true also.* To put it another way, if the premises of a deductively valid argument are true, then its conclusion *cannot be false.*

On the other hand, the premises of an **inductively valid argument** provide good but not conclusive grounds for accepting its conclusion. The truth of its premises does not guarantee the truth of its conclusion, although it does make the conclusion *probable.* (That's why the expression "probability argument" is often used instead of "inductive argument.")

The key idea in induction is that of *learning from experience.* We notice *patterns* or other *resemblances* in our experiences and project them onto other experiences. Here is a typical example:

1. The Indianapolis Colts were a losing team in their first few years of existence.

∴ 2. They'll be a losing team in their next year.

Anyone who accepts this argument's premise (and knows nothing else relevant) is justified in accepting its conclusion. Yet this conclusion *may* turn out to be false. The Colts could conceivably make some inspired trades and draft picks and start playing winning football.

Contrast this inductive argument with the following deductively valid argument:

1. Every U.S. president has lied to us.
2. Jimmy Carter was a U.S. president.

∴ 3. Jimmy Carter lied to us.

Assuming for the moment that the first premise is true (we all know that the second premise is true), it is inconceivable that the conclusion could be false. It would be inconsistent (contradictory) to believe both premises yet deny the conclusion. For in saying the two premises, we have implicitly said the conclusion.

We have here a fundamental difference between deductive and inductive reasoning: The conclusion of a deductively valid argument is just as certain as its premises, while the conclusion of an inductively valid argument is less certain than its premises. Inductive conclusions have that extra element of doubt, however slight, because they make claims not already made by their premises. In contrast, the conclusion of a deductively valid argument is no more doubtful than its premises because its conclusion is already contained in its premises, although often only implicitly. (Deduction and induction, and good reasoning in general, are discussed further in the Appendix, bad or fallacious reasoning in Chapters 2, 3, and 4.)

4. Background Beliefs and World Views

Background beliefs are crucial in assessing argument cogency. Untrue background beliefs lead to errors of the kind many Americans made in 1972 and 1973 when evi-

Valid
What is deductive arg? If prems true, then conclusion true
What is valid ind. arg? If prems true, conclusion probably true
What is difference ded + ind valid arg?
Ded — conclusion as certain as prems
Ind — concl less certain

summary of the entire reading in your notebook. Use both your summary and your underlined text when you review.

This method incorporates fewer of the basic principles than SQ3R. It will give you a familiarity with what you read, but not knowledge in depth. If familiarity is good enough for your task at hand, use it.

Figure 8.2 *Textbook annotation: 3R method*

3. Two Basic Kinds of Valid Arguments

Philosophers have distinguished two basic kinds of correct or valid arguments: **deductive** and **inductive.** The essential property of a **deductively valid argument** is this: *If its premises are true, then its conclusion must be true also.* To put it another way, if the premises of a deductively valid argument are true, then its conclusion *cannot be false.*

On the other hand, the premises of an **inductively valid argument** provide good but not conclusive grounds for accepting its conclusion. The truth of its premises does not guarantee the truth of its conclusion, although it does make the conclusion *probable.* (That's why the expression "probability argument" is often used instead of "inductive argument.")

The key idea in induction is that of *learning from experience.* We notice *patterns* or other *resemblances* in our experiences and project them onto other experiences. Here is a typical example:

   1. The Indianapolis Colts were a losing team in their first few years of existence.

∴ 2. They'll be a losing team in their next year.

Anyone who accepts this argument's premise (and knows nothing else relevant) is justified in accepting its conclusion. Yet this conclusion *may* turn out to be false. The Colts could conceivably make some inspired trades and draft picks and start playing winning football.

Contrast this inductive argument with the following deductively valid argument:

   1. Every U.S. president has lied to us.
   2. Jimmy Carter was a U.S. president.

∴ 3. Jimmy Carter lied to us.

Assuming for the moment that the first premise is true (we all know that the second premise is true), it is inconceivable that the conclusion could be false. It would be inconsistent (contradictory) to believe both premises yet deny the conclusion. For in saying the two premises, we have implicitly said the conclusion.

We have here a fundamental difference between deductive and inductive reasoning: The conclusion of a deductively valid argument is just as certain as its premises, while the conclusion of an inductively valid argument is less certain than its premises. Inductive conclusions have that extra element of doubt, however slight, because they make claims not already made by their premises. In contrast, the conclusion of a deductively valid argument is no more doubtful than its premises because its conclusion is already contained in its premises, although often only implicitly. (Deduction and induction, and good reasoning in general, are discussed further in the Appendix, bad or fallacious reasoning in Chapters 2, 3, and 4.)

4. Background Beliefs and World Views

Background beliefs are crucial in assessing argument cogency. Untrue background beliefs lead to errors of the kind many Americans made in 1972 and 1973 when evi-

READING FOR THE MAIN IDEA

Sometimes you will need only a general idea about what the text says, or you will have very little time to devote to reading your assignment. In those cases you should read for the main idea. Don't bother with any prereading exercises. Begin reading on the first page of the assignment, and read as quickly as you can. Your goal is to find the main idea of each section you read and mark it. Skip the supplementary stuff—examples, details, explanations, illustrations—and go on to the next main idea.

Most texts are arranged in a hierarchy. There is one main idea for the entire text. The main idea for this text, for instance, is that every student can learn to succeed in college. That main idea is supported by subordinate ideas, each one of which becomes the main idea for a chapter. The main idea for this chapter is that there are many different ways to read your textbooks. Each chapter's main ideas are supported by subordinate ideas, which in turn are the main ideas for sections. Each section is further divided into subheads, each devoted to its own main idea. Finally, subheads are divided into paragraphs, the smallest unit that carries a main idea.

Reading hierarchical texts for the main idea is simple. All you need to do is figure out the structure and then find the main idea for each piece of the structure. If you need to understand most of the text, read each paragraph for the main idea and mark it. If you only need to have a broad grasp of the major points, read faster and only mark the main ideas for each subhead or section.

Some of your texts will be narratives, rather than hierarchies. Novels and short stories, poems, biographies, and memoirs do not lend themselves to chapters, sections, and subheads. You can still read them for the main idea. Look for the main point the author wishes to make and mark it. In novels and poems there may be nothing to mark. Sometimes the main point of a story or a novel is unspoken, and the point of a poem is frequently only suggested in the words. You must infer it and write it in the margin.

You can read a good deal of material in not very much time using this method. As long as you don't have to know a great deal about what you read, it works well. Use it for background reading, for catching up, for surveying books that might serve as sources for a paper, or for courses where your goals are modest. If you need to remember the main ideas you have read for any length of time, write a brief summary of them after you complete your reading. Review that summary before the lecture, before your next reading, and before the exam.

SCANNING FOR ANSWERS

We all look things up from time to time. We look up telephone numbers in the phone book, baseball scores in the newspaper, words in a dictionary, data in tables, names in indexes, and so on. The same scanning techniques you use for looking things up can help you in your reading for your courses.

Suppose you are reviewing your geology text for an exam. You can't remember when the theory of tectonic plates was first proposed or who proposed it. Your professor, who is interested in the history of geology as well as the science of geology itself, is likely to ask a few short-answer questions about who proposed the theory. How do you find out? The hard way is to reread the chapter on tectonic plates. You've already read it, and you remember most of it; why take the time? The simple way is to scan through the chapter looking for names and dates—any names, any dates. When you come across either one, read the surrounding text to see if it provides the information you need. If it does, stop; if it doesn't, scan on. Mark the text, in case you have to look it up again, and write what you have learned in your notes for later review.

Or suppose you are considering writing a paper on one of your favorite novels, *The Grapes of Wrath*, for a course on American fiction of the depression era. You want to see if you can relate the novel to some of Steinbeck's own experiences. How do you find out whether or not you can do that? First, look up Steinbeck in an encyclopedia; you'll find that *The Grapes of Wrath* was published in 1939 and that it won both the National Book Award and the Pulitzer Prize for fiction. Now look up Steinbeck in *American Writers* or some other reference work and scan for "1939," "depression," "*The Grapes of Wrath*," "National Book Award," and "Pulitzer Prize." Whatever passages are relevant to your inquiry will probably include at least one of those words or phrases. Read those passages. Finally, find a biography of Steinbeck and scan it in the same way.

Whenever you are reading to answer a question, you can scan. If you need to know how to compute standard deviation for your statistics homework, scan the index or table of contents of your text for "standard deviation," turn to the passage, and scan it for an example. If you need to know the details of the treaty that ended the war against Japan in 1945, scan your history text for that famous photograph of Emperor Hirohito signing a treaty on the deck of the battleship *Missouri*. If you need to know the specific gravity of mercury, scan your chemistry text for the appropriate table, and then scan the table.

In your journal, list your classes and briefly describe the sort of reading assignments you have received in each one. Now decide which of the reading methods listed earlier is appropriate to each class and your goals for it. Write that method next to the class. Finally, use the method you have chosen at least once in completing your reading assignment. Was that method more or less successful than the way you used to read?

Reading Notes

You have already learned that you should always read with a pencil in your hand in order to keep yourself actively involved in your reading. In addition, what you write with your pencil can help you review later on. But don't forget that the primary reason for writing anything anywhere while you are reading is to keep yourself involved. So don't let your note taking distract you from your reading.

What should you write? Whatever helps you concentrate and whatever helps you review. Some students find that underlining and writing cryptic notes in the margin are enough; others find that they must write summaries in their notebooks. The most successful students vary their note-taking techniques, depending on the nature of the course and its reading assignments and on their goals.

The note-taking methods you find most helpful for recording lectures are probably the ones you will find most helpful for recording your readings. If you write your lecture notes in narrative form, your reading notes should probably be in narrative form also. But don't try to write everything down; it will take forever, and you will merely duplicate the text. For an important text in an important course, write sentences to summarize paragraphs and paragraphs to summarize sections. For a less important text or course, write even less.

If you write your lecture notes in outline form, try the same technique for your reading notes. Outlining is hard and time-consuming work, however; few texts are worth the effort it takes to write a complete and accurate outline. For most texts, and for most purposes, partial outlines are sufficient. Each section gets a main heading, with a few subordinate points as subheads and an illustrative detail or two to serve as examples.

The danger with outlining is that you tend to get carried away and find a place in your outline for every bit of information the author provides. Remember that you are doing this reading for your own purposes, not the author's. Only include in your outline the information that is relevant to your own goals. A good way to discipline yourself when outlining is to do your writing in the margin of the text instead of in your notebook. If you write small and abbreviate, you can capture what is essential in your reading in a very narrow space.

Some students write their reading notes in the form of questions, especially if they are using the SQ3R method. As they read each paragraph or section, they invent a question that gets to the heart of the passage and write it down. When reviewing, they ask themselves the questions. If they can answer them, they know the material. This technique works particularly well when the questions are written in the margin of the text; simply cover the printed words with your hand when you review.

This trick can also work if you write extensive notes in a notebook. The first time you review your notes, generate questions about the material and write them in the margin of your notes. The next time you review, cover your notes and ask yourself the questions.

With some texts, the best way to capture the meaning of what you read is to draw a map. Suppose your text for Modern American History devotes a chapter to the Vietnam War. The chapter is organized by the chronology of major events, with explanatory material attached to each event. The simplest way to take notes on this chapter is to chart a timeline. Draw a line across the top of a page in your notebook. Label the left edge "1954—French defeated, depart" and the right edge "1975—South Vietnam surrenders, U.S. departs." In between, write the important dates and events in chronological order. On the rest of the page list details or explanations, attaching them with lines to the appropriate major events on your timeline. The resulting chart maps out in visible form the most important bits of information from the chapter.

Maps can also be used to connect ideas. The Kahane text from Figures 8.1 and 8.2, for instance, is easily amenable to idea mapping, as shown in Figure 8.3. The map contains all of the crucial information: definitions of the two kinds of valid arguments, significant differences between them, and examples.

Mapping creates a visual representation of the connections among facts or ideas. When you look at the map you see not only the facts

Figure 8.3 *Idea mapping*

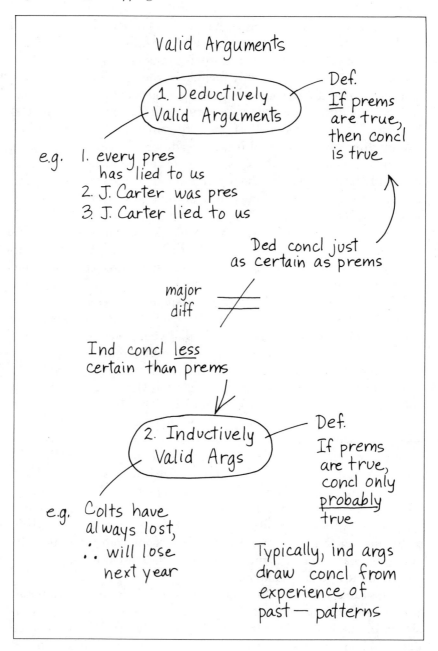

Valid Arguments

1. Deductively Valid Arguments

Def.
If prems are true, then concl is true

e.g. 1. every pres has lied to us
2. J. Carter was pres
3. J. Carter lied to us

Ded concl just as certain as prems

major diff ≠

Ind concl less certain than prems

2. Inductively Valid Args

Def.
If prems are true, concl only probably true

e.g. Colts have always lost, ∴ will lose next year

Typically, ind args draw concl from experience of past — patterns

or ideas you need to remember, but also the ways in which they are related to one another. Consequently you will be able to remember them better on the test. And if your instructor asks you to connect two ideas ("Compare and contrast the teleological theories of Mill and Rawls"), the map you made in your notebook will have given you a head start.

Mapping takes a little more time than scribbling in margins or writing brief summaries. On the other hand, mapping forces you to come to grips with the material you read. In order to draw a map, you must understand not only the facts and ideas you are recording, but also how they are connected. Maps are especially effective for visual learners. If you can't remember anything unless you see it on paper, if your eyes are your favorite route for information, maps can be an extremely powerful tool for you.

EXERCISE 8.3

What is the most demanding textbook you must read? The next time you read a chapter in that text, map it in your notebook. Did mapping contribute to your understanding of the chapter? Will it make that chapter easier to remember? Are the benefits worth the time it took to make the map?

Integrating Reading and Lecture Notes

In most classes, your professor expects you to learn what he thinks is important. Some of it will come from his lectures, some from the text. But on the exam, there is no way to separate lecture material from textbook material. Suppose your English literature professor had you read *Sir Gawain and the Green Knight* and then provided you with some background material on epic poems in class. On the test he may ask you to analyze the role of the hero of *Sir Gawain* in terms of the great tradition of epic poetry in Nordic lands. Just reading the poem will not prepare you to do that, nor will listening to the lecture. You must integrate both reading and lecture into your understanding.

How do you do that? There are some basic rules: You must read the text and listen to the lectures, for starters. Many students think that they can get by in a course just by doing one or the other. Seldom true. Second, you must exercise your mind a little. Consciously relate what you hear in class to the reading you did the night before. And as you read, draw mental connections to what you have been hearing in class.

Chapter 7 suggested some ways to integrate supplementary material with your lecture notes. Count your reading notes as supplementary material, and build them all together. If your reading notes consist of underlinings and margin notes in the text, write a brief summary of what you have read in your lecture notebook. If your reading notes consist of a set of questions, write them in the margins of your lecture notes. If you have drawn a map of your reading, paper clip it to your lecture notes. Whatever you do, make sure that you review all of your notes at the same time.

But just looking at your various notes at the same time will get you nowhere. You must integrate them in your head in order to perform on the exam. When you review, don't just read over your notes until they sink in. Read them critically, and look for the arguments. Ask questions as you review: Why did the Nordic lands produce so many epics? What makes Gawain a hero? What are the connections between *Sir Gawain* and *Beowulf*, between the British and Icelandic sagas, between middle English literature and Wagner? Asking yourself questions will force you to combine the information you have gathered from each source. The exam will ask you to do that anyway; doing it while you review will give you a head start.

Just before class, review both your lecture notes from the previous class and your reading notes for the day's reading assignment. Reviewing both sets of notes at the same time will help you combine them in your mind.

Take a practice test. Invent a few questions typical of the exams you have seen so far. Better yet, invent some questions with a study partner and trade. As you write the answers, draw upon your recollections of both lectures and the text. When you are done, review your answers with a critical eye to see how they might be improved (better yet, have your study partner do it for you), and go back to your lecture or reading notes to fill in the gaps.

EXERCISE 8.4

How are you currently integrating the information you gather from your texts with what you hear in your lectures? Does your method work well enough to help you meet your goals? Write the answers to these questions in your journal, and speculate on how you might do a better job of integration.

Summary

This chapter taught you how to read your texts. Read them actively, with a pencil in your hand. Know as much as you can about the passage before you begin reading it. Adjust your reading speed and concentration to match the level of difficulty of the text, the nature of the assignment, and your own goals. Write a brief summary after you read. Look for the arguments in your text.

There are various methods you can follow as you read: SQ3R, 3R, reading for the main idea, and scanning for answers. There are various techniques for taking notes on your reading: underlining, margin notes, narratives, outlines, and questions. However you read your texts, however you take notes upon your reading, you must integrate what you learn from your texts with what you learn from lectures. Physically integrating your notes can help, but the crucial step is integrating them in your head.

No one can practice all of these various tricks. Find the ones that help you reach your goals and incorporate them into your study routines.

9

Learning Through Experience

You have been learning through experience since the day you were born. You learned the consequences of touching a hot stove through experience. You learned how to skip rope and throw a baseball through experience. You learned to dance through experience. Most of your learning outside of school has been experiential learning.

But even in school, some of what you learned came through direct experience. In your high school biology course you learned how frogs are put together by actually dissecting them. In auto mechanics and keyboarding and wood shop, you learned by digging into engines or typing or working on a lathe. You learned about theater by acting in plays and building scenery. You learned about athletics by participating.

Some of your coursework in college will depend on experiential learning too. You will probably take at least one laboratory course, in which you learn the basics of chemistry or physics partly by mucking about in the lab. You may engage in an internship or cooperative education program, in which you apply the theoretical knowledge you gained in the classroom to real-world, working situations. Your major might require some sort of field experience such as student teaching, in which you actually practice what your professors have been teaching you.

All of these sorts of experiences will give you a wonderful opportunity to learn—as long as you approach them with the proper attitude. Too many students think of them as just another requirement, like the requirement to pass a swimming test or to earn a C in English Composition. Not so; these activities are integral to your education. This chapter will show you how to take advantage of them.

Experiential Learning

Remember how you learned to ride a bicycle? You probably started by observing the actions of someone else riding a bicycle, or perhaps listening to your dad's instructions ("Start with one foot on the ground and one on the upper pedal; now push down on the pedal, and raise your other foot at the same time—don't forget to steer!"). Then you tried it yourself, doubtless scraping your knee when your bike tipped over. As you lay on the ground you reflected on why it didn't work. Your dad may have had some helpful words of advice as well— "No, no, you have to steer in the direction you start to fall." You tried again, and this time you got halfway down the block before you fell into the hedge. Once again you thought about what happened and realized that steering helps keep you balanced. And so you kept at it, refining your notions about riding a bicycle through your actual experience. Before long you could ride anywhere.

You followed a similar process when you learned to balance a checkbook, swim, or write book reports. First you formed a beginning hypothesis about how to start, either through observing someone else doing it or through listening to an explanation from someone who knew how. Then you tried it, failed, modified your hypothesis, tried again, expanded your hypothesis, did it some more, and so on. Theory and practice were both essential elements of this sequence. You couldn't learn without forming some hypotheses in your mind —that's the theory. You couldn't learn without trying your theory out—that's the practice.*

Many, perhaps most, of your classes in college are primarily theoretical. Your instructors will lecture to you and have you read lots of books. They will expect you to learn the general principles of their disciplines so you can answer questions on exams correctly and write papers coherently. However, some of your classes will build an experiential dimension into the coursework. Take advantage of them.

----

*For a more complete explanation of experiential learning, see David Kolb, *Experiential Learning: Experience as the Source of Learning and Development*, Englewood Cliffs, NJ, Prentice-Hall, 1984.

One of the themes of this book is that *all* learning follows the theory–practice model and that you can get the most out of your college experience by connecting the theory you learn to your own experiences. (See Chapter 3.) You should apply the political theory you learn in political science to the politics you see in your communities or residence halls. You should personalize the ethical theory you learn in philosophy by thinking about your own ethical dilemmas in their terms. You should flesh out the theories of classification you learn in biology by naming the plants you see as you walk around campus. And so on. These activities will help you learn the theory, just as trying out your bicycle helped you learn how to ride.

Laboratory Courses

Many science courses include laboratories. You will probably take at least one of them to complete the general education requirements at your college. Many students dislike labs. They're messy, they smell bad, they make you get your hands dirty, and they seldom turn out the way they're supposed to. Others absolutely love them, for exactly the same reasons. In any case, you must take them. You might as well get as much out of them as you can.

There are some general principles you should follow when taking a laboratory course.

PREPARE

Students who dislike labs have a tendency to walk into them expecting the instructor to tell them everything they need to know. That works in lectures, after all; why shouldn't it work in labs? Because labs are different from lectures. In lectures you receive information passively. Preparing for a lecture (by reviewing notes from the previous lecture, by doing the reading assignments in advance) contributes to your understanding, as I have argued elsewhere in this book, but it's not crucial. In labs you are actively involved in what's going on. That's how you get your hands dirty. Doing some preparation gets you involved before you actually walk into the laboratory; that way you can take maximum advantage of your limited lab time.

How do you prepare for a lab? First, read the lab assignment. Lab instructors almost always give you a lab assignment before the lab. It will tell you the purpose of the lab, the protocol for you to follow, some warnings about potential hazards, and the assignment for your lab report. Many students don't read their lab assignments until they are standing at the lab bench ready to start. Big mistake. They should be using that time doing the experiment.

Think about the experiment you are about to do while you are reading the lab assignment; to help you think, write in your notebook or journal. Formulate a clear idea of the purpose of the experiment: to learn the musculature of the cat; to discover the relationship among ohms, watts, and amperes; to identify a series of rock samples; to classify a chemical compound. Write that purpose down. Go over the procedure you will follow. Try to understand the purpose of each step and write it down. Note the hazards. Understand what sort of data you must record for your lab report, and set up the tables or charts you will need to record them.

Spend a few moments placing the lab into the framework of the course as a whole. Why are you learning the musculature of the cat in Biology II? Because the cat's structure is representative of all mammals. Why are you investigating the relationship among watts, ohms, and amperes for Introduction to Physics? Because Ohm's law, the expression of that relationship, is one of the basic laws of physics. Why are you identifying all these rocks for Earth Science 101? Because until you understand the differences among different sorts of rock, you cannot understand how the earth was formed. Why are you classifying a compound in Organic Chemistry? Because that's what organic chemists do.

MAKE THE LAB RELEVANT
TO REAL PROBLEMS

Your understanding of the purpose of the lab and the procedures you follow will be enhanced if you can relate them to something relevant to your life. If you are dissecting a cat, spend some time watching live cats move. Explain to your roommate or spouse or child which muscle groups are at work when Fluffy jumps on the refrigerator. If you are studying Ohm's law, use it to figure how big your stereo speakers can be. If you are identifying rocks, try to connect the samples with actual locations. You might even bring a few samples from your home town to lab and see if the instructor can identify them. If you are classifying organic chemical compounds, imagine how you would go about classifying the various components of your favorite beverage.

We are deluged every day with news of scientific issues that affect the lives of all of us: cold fusion, global warming, ozone depletion, genetic engineering, groundwater pollution. Relating the work you are doing in your lab courses to these issues will bring them alive for you. And you can do that. Cold fusion is basic physical chemistry (with some implications for physicists). Genetic engineering puts to work the concepts you learn in Introductory Biology, and the possibilities for genetically altering organisms permeate every biology course. And so on.

Making the lab relevant to real problems, yours or the world's, will help you in several ways: You'll understand better what you're doing and why you're doing it; you'll remember the procedures you followed and the results you achieved—important if you will be tested on your labs; and you'll enjoy the lab more because it's connected to something real.

TAKE ADVANTAGE
OF YOUR LAB INSTRUCTOR

Most lab courses meet in large lectures several times a week and break into lab sections for experiments. Thus lab sections are relatively small. They are led by a lab instructor. She'll get you started, walk around answering questions, look for potential disasters, and make sure you clean up. You have far more access to your lab instructor than to your lecturer. Take advantage of that access. Ask questions about the lab. Ask questions about how the lab is connected to yesterday's lecture. Ask whether the procedure you're using might be used to solve other problems. Don't monopolize her time, but take advantage of her presence.

OBSERVE EVERYTHING

Most lab experiments follow this model: Initiate change and watch what happens. Because you've already read the lab assignment, you know what's supposed to happen, so you watch for it. But you should watch everything else that's going on too. Sometimes experiments don't work the way you (or your instructor) anticipated. If you have been observant of everything that was going on, you have a good chance of figuring out where the experiment went astray.

Laboratory veterans get in the habit of describing the environment of the experiment in their notebooks before they begin recording their data: "Science Hall room 412, 9 A.M., air temp 37 C, bright sunlight on bench, low humidity." They try to anticipate each variable that may have an effect on the experiment and record it. Try it.

REFLECT ON THE LAB

Write about the lab in your journal or notebook. What do your results mean? What general principles do your results support? Are those general principles—theories—the same as the ones you've been hearing about in the lectures? If not, what might have gotten in the way?

Also reflect on the procedures you followed. What did you learn about scientific method? If things went as planned, your experiment either verified or invalidated some general theory. Will that method of verification or invalidation work in other, nonscientific courses? Think about the laboratory techniques you used: Prepare, keep it clean, observe everything, and so on. Can those techniques be used in other settings?

Finally, reflect on how this lab fits into the course as a whole. What does the musculature of a cat show you about the structure of mammals? How does Ohm's law help tie the physical universe together? What does the difference between igneous and sedimentary rocks tell us about the composition of the world? Will the techniques you used in analyzing this specific chemical compound work for every organic compound? And so on.

Some instructors will tell you some of these principles beforehand, some will not. The set of general directions for a lab in Figure 9.1 comes from an excellent biology instructor. If your lab instructor doesn't give you something like it, adapt it to the lab course you are taking and use it.

Figure 9.1 *Sample laboratory directions* (from Van Gooch, University of Minnesota, Morris)

Standard Lab Considerations in Molecular Biology

I. Be prepared: The procedures you will be using are sequential, and most are time consuming and involve expensive chemicals. One silly mistake can negate the entire procedure and be very costly in terms of time and money. Know what you are doing before you start. You <u>will</u> make mistakes, but try to minimize them.

    1. Have a protocol (a lab assignment).

    2. Understand the protocol.

    3. Have a notebook.

    4. Have all needed solutions prepared.

    5. Know where all needed solutions are.

    6. Know how to use the necessary equipment.

II. Think what you are doing during the experiment.

III. Record what happens in your notebook.

<u>Before</u> the experiment, do the following:

    1. Give the experiment a title.

    2. Date the experiment (usually the starting date).

    3. List your lab partners.

    4. In a section labeled ''PURPOSE,'' write down, in a sentence or two, the purpose of the experiment.

<u>During</u> the experiment:

    1. In a section labeled ''EXPERIMENT,'' write down all pertinent actions, aberrations, etc., as you do the experiment. Observe everything, and record anything that might have an effect on your results.

(continued)

<u>After</u> the experiment:

1. Analyze the data as soon as you can after the experiment. You will probably need to remember some things you forgot to write down, so the sooner the better.

2. Put all tables, pictures, graphs, etc., in your notebook. If appropriate, put this in a section labeled ''RESULTS.''

3. In a section labeled ''CONCLUSION,'' write down a one- or two-sentence conclusion you reached. It must respond to the original purpose, at least in part, though you may draw additional conclusions.

Hints during an experiment:

1. Be conscious of sterility. At every step ask if this needs to be fully sterile, if it needs to be sort of sterile, or if sterility is of no concern. Don't contaminate your cultures. Don't contaminate solutions others will assume to be sterile.

2. Be conscious of temperature. At every step ask if this is okay at room temperature, or should it be on ice, in the freezer, or at 37 C.

3. Keep everything labeled! Use water-insoluble markers. Realize solvents and water can take off markings and tape.

4. Always be prepared to redo an experiment:

   a. Think about each step and what you would do differently if you were to do it over. Make notes in your notebook about such improvements.

   b. Don't discard cultures and solutions that might be valuable in a repeat.

5. Be conscious of safety:

   a. Always wear gloves when working with ethidium bromide or ethidium bromide gels.

   b. Always wear gloves when working with phenol, and work under the hood.

```
c. Avoid bacterial contamination. Wear gloves
   when working with live cultures. Don't spill,
   drop, or splatter cultures; clean them up
   with disinfectant if you do. Put pipette
   tips, Eppendorf tubes, etc., in disinfectant
   when done. Disinfect or sterilize old
   cultures and flasks that had cultures, old
   plates, etc.
```

Internships

Internships are wonderful opportunities to combine the theoretical knowledge you gain in the classroom with the practical knowledge you learn on a job site. In your business classes, you may learn about marketing theories. In an internship with Amalgamated Widgets, you might learn how those theories apply in practice by designing a marketing plan. In Political Science 3402, you may learn how state tax policies are supposed to be created. In an internship with your state legislator, you might learn how that really happens by working on a tax bill. In Organic Chemistry I, you may learn how to analyze the impurities in water. As an intern with your local water pollution agency, you might learn why that's an important skill by analyzing your neighbor's water supplies.

Most internships are academic experiences, designed in conjunction with a faculty member to make sure that you are applying the theory you learned in the classroom. They earn you credit. They conclude with some sort of academic evaluation: a paper, an oral or written examination, or an interview by your faculty supervisor. At the same time they are work experiences. You will have a set of responsibilities assigned to you and a boss who will see that you carry them out. Your work will be evaluated, and (in many cases) you will be on the payroll. You will hang out at the water cooler with the rest of the crew.

The typical internship takes place during the summer between your junior and senior year. Usually the work experience will be related to your major. The pay will be similar to the summer jobs you have had in the past. You'll have a great time while you learn a great deal about your chosen field. And you may impress your supervisor so much that you'll have an inside track on a job when you graduate.

However, many internships do not follow this typical pattern. Some carry no credit. Many take place during the school year. Some students will take a quarter or semester or even an entire year off to do an internship with a senator or with a large corporation. Others will do a part-time internship with a local governmental office while they are taking classes. The work experience may not be related to your major at all. Philosophy majors take internships with real estate companies; geology majors take internships with urban planning agencies; French majors take internships with hospitals. You may not be paid; many nonprofit organizations have little money and cannot pay their interns. You may have a lousy time. Not all internships are successes. You may not gain entry to your eventual employer. In fact, you may decide that you never want to do that sort of work again—a valuable lesson in itself.

Students headed for the human service professions—health services, social agencies, governmental service—typically take internships, sometimes to meet a requirement for graduation. Many business students do internships as a way to impress potential employers. Science students become interns in laboratories to gain research experience. Foreign language students do internships as translators to sharpen their skills. Students in all majors do internships to leaven their classroom experience. For many students, the theory they learn in the classroom is simply too abstract. They need to see practical applications of the theory before it makes sense. Internships are excellent ways to gather that practical knowledge.

Some internships are thoroughly organized. The Cooperative Education Program, funded by the U.S. Department of Education, sends students to a job site for a semester, back to campus for more coursework, and then to the job site again for a more advanced work experience. Coop Ed internships usually pay well and frequently lead to a job offer. At the other end of the scale are the informal internships many students arrange on their own: summer work with an employer in a field of interest, a part-time campus job doing library research for a professor in the discipline they plan to pursue in graduate school, an independent study experience investigating the practical implications of a theory they learned in a particular class.

No matter which of these patterns you adopt, there are some general principles you should follow in setting up an internship.

START NOW

Begin thinking about internships now, even if you are only a freshman. Visit the office in your college that helps arrange internships. Large schools usually have an internship coordinator; smaller schools coordinate internships through their placement centers. Pick up the brochures describing internships, check out the listings of openings available today, introduce yourself to the staff, and tell them you are browsing. Talk to your instructors about the possibility of internships in their fields. Talk to your adviser about the advisability of internships in your major and in your intended occupation. Talk to your parents or your partner about the financial implications of devoting a summer or some school time to an internship. Begin making lists of possible areas of interest, possible job sites, possible employers. Ask those employers whether they ever hire interns. If they don't know what you're talking about, explain the concept to them.

At the same time, think about how practical experience can verify or invalidate the theories you are learning in the classroom. When you are learning about competing theories of psychoanalysis, for instance, imagine how you would use them with clients. As you investigate the principles of international finance, imagine how you would put those principles to work if you were handling currency exchanges in a New York bank. These mental experiments will help get you ready for your internship and help you understand and remember the material.

WORK CLOSELY WITH YOUR FACULTY SUPERVISOR

Before you start your internship, reach an agreement with a faculty member on what you intend to get out of your internship. Think about exactly how your practical experience is going to fill out your theoretical knowledge. Set some specific learning goals, and design a way to measure whether or not you have met the goals you jointly design. With a credit-bearing internship, the structures your college imposes upon you should ensure that you work closely with your faculty supervisor so you can earn your credits. But even if your internship will be an informal one—a summer job in your field or part-time campus work—make sure that you and your faculty adviser both understand what you hope to gain.

MONITOR YOUR PROGRESS

During your internship, make sure that it is contributing to your learning goals, whatever they are. If your law office supervisor has you doing nothing but printing form letters to clients, you are probably not learning very much about personal injury suits. If the art museum has you spend all of your time sweeping floors, you will learn little about restoring pre-Columbian pottery. If the Sanitary District has you digging ditches, you probably will not be able to flesh out your theoretical knowledge of modern sewage handling techniques. Speak up; most internships are built on a premise of combining academic and real-world experience. If the combination is not there, consult with both your faculty and work site supervisors.

Most employers enter into internship agreements because they believe in their value as combinations of work and school. If the combination is not working, they will usually modify the experience so that it does. A few employers think of interns as cheap labor. That's not necessarily bad, as long as what you are learning is worth what you are giving up in income. If it's not, change it.

REFLECT ON YOUR WORK EXPERIENCE

The point of an internship is to bring your theoretical knowledge to bear on actual problems, thereby enriching what you know. In order to make that happen, you have to think about what you are doing. While you are analyzing water samples, think about the chemistry behind the technique. While you are computing exchange rates, think about the economic principles that explain their fluctuations. While you are designing marketing plans, think about the psychological theories underlying them. A structured internship will force you to reflect in these ways through the evaluation device at the end. If you are in a less formal internship, you may have to remind yourself to reflect on your experience. Or ask your faculty adviser to remind you.

How do you go about getting an internship? Basically there are two ways: letting your college arrange it for you and setting it up on your own. Most schools have an office that handles internships. Some have full-time coordinators who beat the bushes for opportunities for their students. Others simply take listings over the phone and post them. In either case, scan the possibilities and pursue the ones that interest you. Alternatively, you can set up your own internship. You may think of a potential employer, or one might be suggested to you by an instructor, a parent, or a friend. Sometimes your current employer might be a possibility. Ask: Do you sponsor interns? If they do, follow up with the intern coordinator at your college or with an instructor.

You can learn all sorts of things through internships. Applying or arranging for one will sharpen your job-seeking skills: filling out applications, interviewing, following up. And an internship will teach you a great deal about the working world. In college if you are a little late to class, or with an assignment, the world doesn't end. On the job, being late can be much more serious. In college, what you wear or say or how you act seldom counts; on the job, it frequently does. An internship will sometimes demonstrate that a particular field is right (or wrong) for you. But the major benefit of an internship is combining theoretical with practical knowledge.

EXERCISE 9.2

In your journal, design an internship for yourself for next summer. First, name the job site and describe the sort of work you will do. Second, outline the academic component. What will you learn? How will your learning be evaluated? Who will be your faculty supervisor? Third, what steps should you take between now and next summer to make it happen?

If the internship you have designed looks attractive to you, invent it by following the steps you outlined.

Field Learning

Many programs and majors require their students actually to work in the field before they can graduate. The best-known example is teacher education, which requires students to do several months of actual teaching while they are undergraduates. Most states require teachers-to-be to demonstrate their competence through a successful student teaching experience before they can be licensed. Other undergraduate programs that frequently require a field experience are the health sciences (physical and occupational and respiratory therapy, nursing, medical technology, exercise physiology, and so on), law, and social work.

Many of these programmatic requirements are actually state requirements. Where a job requires a license, the state frequently requires a field-learning experience so students can demonstrate that they know the basic standards of the profession.

Like internships, field-learning experiences give students the opportunity to apply the theories they have learned in the classroom to practical situations. Education students learn a great deal of theory about how classroom instruction should work. As student teachers, they can try out those theories on living students. Physical therapy students memorize the physiology of the human body. In their field experience, they put that knowledge to work by rehabilitating injured athletes.

And, like internships, field-learning experiences give you the chance to try out your chosen profession. They put you on the firing line: Student teachers actually teach classes, physical therapists knead muscles, social workers work with indigent clients, and so on. Most students love it, but a few decide that they really don't like that sort of work after all. It's better to find that out while you are still an undergraduate and can alter your program than after you graduate.

Field-learning experiences seldom include an academic component. You will probably not have to write a paper or take an examination after you complete your assignment, as you would with an internship. However, most field experiences do carry academic credit. Usually your field supervisor and a professor from your program will jointly evaluate your work to see that you have earned the credit.

The same basic principles hold for field-learning experiences as for internships: Start planning early in your undergraduate career; work closely with both your adviser and field supervisor; monitor your progress to make sure you are learning what you need to learn; and reflect on your field experience while you are on the job and after you complete it.

Field-learning experiences are usually an integral part of a major or a program. Consequently you will probably not have to make the arrangements yourself, as you might with an internship. Some colleges have an office that coordinates all field-learning experiences, and others leave it up to individual departments. Ask your adviser if your major requires or encourages field learning; she'll tell you all you need to know.

Summary

Psychologists tell us that all learning combines theory and experience. But some learning is heavily experiential—learning to shoot marbles, learning to drive a car. Other learning is heavily theoretical—

learning to analyze poetry, learning to factor equations. Most of your coursework is heavily theoretical. Elsewhere in this book I have argued that you will learn the most and the fastest in those theoretical classes as you apply the theory to situations that mean something to you. This chapter has described some learning opportunities available to you that are heavily experiential.

Take advantage of them. Think of the laboratory course you are required to take as an opportunity to check out those scientific theories you've been learning in class. Think of the summer internship your adviser talked you into as an opportunity to verify the basic principles of your discipline—and to explore a possible career. Think of the field-learning experience your major requires before you graduate as an opportunity to put those theoretical principles you've been memorizing to work in real situations.

Learning
Through Practice

With many courses, if you understand the basic concepts you understand the course—and you earn good grades. In Introduction to Ethics, for instance, if you can grasp the meanings of Aristotle's golden mean and Kant's categorical imperative, you can perform well on the essay exam. In American Political Systems, if you understand the basic structure of a representative democracy, you can outline it on the test.

But in some courses, understanding the basic concepts is not enough. In calculus, for instance, understanding the basic principles will get you nowhere on the exam—you have to be able to work the problems to pass. In Accounting I, having a basic grasp of the double-entry system of bookkeeping will not suffice—you must be able to use it. Knowing what a five-paragraph essay is will not bring you success in a composition class—you must write good papers. Learning the grammatical structure of Spanish or Chinese or Russian will help you on some of your tests, but it won't give you a speaking knowledge. In all of these courses, understanding the theory is not enough. You must perform in order to succeed.

Most of your outside-of-class activities require more than theoretical knowledge as well. In choir and band, understanding harmonies is useless unless you can perform. It's the same in athletics. If knowledge of the basic principles of sports were enough, armchair quarterbacks would be all-stars. If you can't perform, you won't make the team.

149

To be able to perform in these courses and activities, you must be able to do more than just repeat concepts; you must perform. Being able to perform means practicing. This chapter will show you how to go about it.

Mathematics Courses

Many students have difficulty with math courses. In fact, some students think that the ability to do math is genetically programmed into some people and not into others; if you don't have the math gene, you just can't do math. Not so. There is no math gene. The differences between those who are good at math and those who are not is a matter of behavior. And behavior can be learned.

I've known many students who entered college with fear and loathing for math, convinced that they couldn't possibly do it. But the programs of study they had planned required math, to their dismay. So we changed their behavior, and they tried it again. Most succeeded; a few have become math majors.

The key is practice. Lots of practice. If you have ever taken music lessons, been in theater, or been on an athletic team, you know that you simply cannot succeed without practice. You can't play the guitar unless you do it a lot; you can't learn to juggle without constant repetition; you can't develop a consistent jump shot or curve ball without practicing.

In math, you can't expect to be able to factor equations on an exam unless you have practiced a lot *before* the exam. You can't find derivatives or solve word problems or apply a T-test unless you have rehearsed a great deal beforehand. You simply can't perform unless you practice. Fortunately, math instructors usually give you plenty of opportunities to practice. That's what homework assignments are for. And you can invent some additional means of practicing for yourself.

HOMEWORK

The most important thing with homework, of course, is to do it. Students in college math classes are sometimes tempted not to do their math homework. Instructors don't always collect it; when they bother to collect it, they don't always check it. And even when they check it, homework usually doesn't count for much toward the final grade. So it's easy to say to yourself, "I'll skip this problem set tonight; I understand what's going on, and I really have to start my English paper." Big mistake. Skipping math homework is as damaging to a math student as skipping practice is to a basketball player. You miss a wonderful opportunity to prepare for the performance—the test or the game.

The best time to do your math homework is immediately after your math class, or at least in your first available free hour. The demonstrations you saw on the board are still fresh in your mind; the explanations are still current; and if you get stuck you have time to do something about it. The worst time to do math homework, for most people, is just before it's due. Still, it's better to do it then than not at all.

Many students treat their math homework as drudgery. They sigh a lot, their minds wander, they crank up the TV, and they grind away at their problems until they get the answers. They don't learn much. (They didn't learn much on the piano when they approached their music lessons in the same way, either.) The aim is *not* to get the answers; the aim is to practice solving these sorts of problems so that you can get the answer on the exam. Think of math homework as studying for the test. That should make it easier to concentrate.

In order to get anything out of your math homework, you must be conscious of what you are doing while you work your problems. If you can solve a problem easily, make sure you understand what you did. ("Okay, first I got rid of the parentheses by multiplying this guy throughout; then I divided by this guy from over here; then I subtracted, and that isolated the *X*.") Guessing the answer or doing it unconsciously won't do you any good—even if you get it right. Many students will work at a problem until they have an answer, check it against the answers in the back of the book, see that it's right, and stop. But unless they know how they got that answer—unless they reflect on the method they used—their work will not do them much good on the exam.

If you can't solve the problem easily, you'll learn more. When you struggle with a problem, you tend to concentrate on it. And when you concentrate, you tend to remember. Still, you must be aware of the steps you take in solving it. After you have come to a solution, review what you did. Try and generate some general principles. ("I see how it works; when I'm given speed, distance, and starting time, I can figure out exactly where the train will be at any specified time.") Try out those general principles on the next problem to make sure they work.

As you are solving a problem, check your work. Does the answer you get at each step seem reasonable? Is your arithmetic correct? Have you lost a sign? Checking as you go along will help you reach a correct answer, and it's good practice for the exam. More important, it will help you watch what you are doing; when you watch what you are doing, you remember what you did.

Once you have completed your homework, think about it a little. How do these problems relate to real life? Who would ever use these techniques on the job? Do the general principles used in solving these problems have any application in my other courses? Reflecting on your math homework in this way will help you see its relevance to your life. That will help you remember how to solve these problems when you see them on the exam.

You should also play with your homework problems once you have completed them. After you have solved a problem, change it around and solve it again. Change the numbers, the variables, or the assumptions. Rewrite word problems so that what you are given comes in a different order, or leave out one of the premises to see if you could still solve it. Some students work their problems backwards once they have solved them: "Let's see, if I were given the time of day the train arrived at its destination and its average speed, what could I infer about when it left Grand Central?" Playing with your problems in these ways will help you get used to seeing a variety of problems and will help you seize instantly the appropriate technique to solve them.

Many students who do fine on their homework do poorly on exams. "The problems look different," they say. Of course they look different. No instructor is going to test you with problems you've already seen. Playing with your homework problems will help you transfer your homework success to test-taking success.

If you think that the homework your instructor is assigning does not give you enough practice, go in search of more. Find an old textbook in the library and work some of the problems in it. Or ask your instructor; she'll be happy to give you some more problems to practice on, and she'll be impressed by your initiative.

READING

Many students use their math textbooks as nothing more than a volume of problems. For information about how to solve the problems, they rely on the instructor's lectures and demonstrations. Big mistake. Your text is a wonderful place to learn problem-solving techniques, to learn math theory, and to learn about the applications of the techniques you are learning. Unfortunately, you may not find it very easy to use.

Reading a math text is very different from reading a philosophy or history text. You can't recline on the sofa with your algebra book propped on your stomach, sip a soft drink, listen to the news with one ear, and expect to learn any algebra. In order to learn anything from a math text you have to go very slowly, concentrate hard, and use your pencil.

Suppose your instructor tells you to read sections 1–3 of Chapter 7 and do the odd-numbered problems. The best way for most students to do this assignment is to read the assigned sections *before* the professor lectures on it. Read slowly and with your pencil in your hand. In most math texts, each paragraph presents one idea. Make sure you understand that idea before you go on. Look at the charts and diagrams and graphs, and work out any examples yourself. That way you internalize what you are reading. Now go to the next paragraph and follow the same process. It may take you an hour or more to read a ten-page section following this method and more time to work the problems. But you'll understand what you've read, and you'll be able to remember it when you take the exam.

There's an alternative method: Start with the problems, and refer back to the text as needed to find explanations, demonstrations, and examples. The advantage of this method is that you will probably get through your homework more quickly; the disadvantage is that you will probably not understand very much of what you did. In order to grasp the concepts behind the techniques you have used to solve the problems, read the sections afterwards. It won't take you long—you have already seen most of the text—and it will pay off enormously in your understanding.

A second alternative: Put your homework off until *after* you hear the lecture. Once you hear what the instructor says, the text will make much better sense to you, and the problems will be much easier to solve. The advantage of this method is the time you save. The disadvantage is that you are in serious danger of falling behind. If the instructor's explanation was a little unclear and you just can't understand the text at all when you read it after class, you have no recourse. You can't ask the instructor to clarify it during class the next day; he's already on the next section.

If you must follow this method, make sure you have some backup help: a tutor, a roommate or friend who has already taken the course, a tolerant instructor with lots of office hours. And do whatever you must to catch up. Falling behind in math can be fatal.

PERSISTENCE

With math, as with any skill requiring practice, you have to persist. You might be able to skip your other courses for days, or even weeks, without hurting your grade. In math class, if you skip a day you are likely to be lost when you return. Mathematics courses are almost always cumulative; what you learn one day is the basis for what you will learn the next. So if you miss a day, you may have missed the crucial bit of information on which the rest of the course is built. That makes it hard to catch up.

You also have to persist in your studying. The biggest difference I have seen between those who can do math and those who say they cannot is that the first group never gives up on a problem. If they can't solve it one way, they'll try another. If that doesn't work, they'll go in search of some help. Even math teachers get stuck on problems. But they persist until they find a solution. So when your homework is tough, you have to keep going. When you just can't solve the problem, find some help. Remind yourself that your instructor is likely to put a problem just like that one on the exam.

STUDY GROUPS

You've already read in this book that study groups are a wonderful way to learn. They work especially well in math. Study groups help keep you honest. It's easy to fool yourself into thinking that you learned something by racing through a problem and checking the answer against the back of the book. It's harder to fool your colleagues in a study group. "Wait a minute," they'll say; "how'd you get that answer? How would you solve this problem if we divided all the quantities by 2? Is a problem like this one likely to be on the test?"

Study groups can be as small as two or as large as six; if they get larger than that, they tend to degenerate. The group should have a common purpose: to ace the exam, or learn enough to get by, or be ready for the math portion of the GRE. And all members should participate more or less equally. Sometimes students want to join just to listen. It doesn't work. They don't learn much from listening—we all learn more math from doing it than from hearing about it—and eventually everyone else will get annoyed at the freeloaders.

Some groups are highly structured. Each member will work through a problem out loud until he gets stuck; then the next person takes over. Others are less formal. Some groups simply gather at the same time every day to do their homework together. When someone gets stuck, she'll ask for help. Some students form study groups to prepare for tests. Two or more students will write sample questions for each other and then solve them. Then they'll discuss how they solved them, why they selected those questions, and how likely it is that questions like those might appear on the exam. How you structure your study group matters less than that you do it.

Some schools will help you set up a study group. Tutoring programs, in effect, give you another person to study with. Sometimes you will be assigned a tutor for the duration of the course—a permanent study group. Other schools offer a drop-in help center for math—a temporary study group. Some math instructors build small group experiences into their courses—in-class study groups. Even if your school doesn't offer any assistance in forming study groups, you can still set one up on your own. Most times they are more effective than anything your institution can invent.

PRACTICE TESTS

Football teams usually scrimmage before games; theater groups always have a dress rehearsal before the first performance; choral groups typically run through a concert the night before they give it. You should prepare for an exam by taking a practice test. Taking a practice test will ease some of the pressure you might otherwise feel on test day. Practice tests will also show you where your weaknesses are in time to do something about them.

One way to practice for a test is to write and take practice questions with your study group, as described earlier. Another way is to ask your instructor for some old tests you can use for practice. Some schools require instructors to deposit their old exams in a central location: the library, the math assistance center, or the tutoring room. Find out if your school has that policy; if it does, take advantage of it.

No matter where you find your practice test, try to take it at least 24 hours before the exam. Better yet, 48 hours. If you take a practice test the same day as the genuine test, the pressure will already be on; the practice will do little to ease it. And there won't be time enough to do much studying to build up your weak areas.

The best practice tests duplicate, as much as possible, the actual testing situation: time limits, silence, even a similar room. Sometimes that's not feasible. Study groups frequently take informal practice tests as part of their sessions instead.

No matter where or how you take your test, spend some time afterward reflecting on it. What sorts of questions were easiest for you to solve? Which ones were hardest? Why were they so hard? Did you not know how to start? Did you not know the appropriate formulas? Did you make dumb mistakes? Did you fail to check your work? If you are working in a group, do your reflecting out loud. Your colleagues will help you figure out some strategies for improvement in your weak areas.

Once you have figured out *what* you need to improve, spend some time improving it. If you don't know how to start on a particular sort of problem, or if you don't know which formula to use, get some help from your instructor or a tutor or your study group. If you made dumb mistakes, make sure you know what they were. Resolve to check your work on the exam. And work more problems like the ones that gave you trouble: practice, practice, practice.

PREPARING FOR EXAMS

Every time you solve homework problems, you are studying for the exam. Every time your study group speculates on what might be on the test, you are preparing for it. Every time you go over yesterday's quiz with your roommate, you are studying for the final. Still, you should do some extra review before a test or exam.

Make sure you are caught up *before* you begin reviewing. Some students put off their homework assignments until the night before the test, thinking that solving the problems will teach them all they need to know. "Besides," they say, "if I do my homework the night before, the problems will be fresh in my mind, right?" Well, they might be. But you're not going to see those problems on the test; you're going to see somewhat different ones. In order to know how to solve those different problems, you must grasp the general principles of solving them. And it's hard to grasp those general principles by starting the night before. Besides, suppose you *can't* solve them the night before the test. At that point, no one can help you. So catch up on your math before you start reviewing. Better yet, keep up as you go along.

A colleague who teaches math recommends following this sequence in preparing for a big math exam: Three or 4 days before the test, spend several hours reviewing all of the material that will be covered. Try to get a general idea of how the different concepts and techniques are connected to one another. In your notebook or journal write down all of the formulas you'll need to know, and add some problems illustrating how those formulas are used. The next day, spend an hour or three condensing what you wrote the day before. The day before the exam, condense it again into the most critical formulas. Don't study just before the exam, he says; what you cram into your head will displace what you've already put there. Following this system got him through both undergraduate and graduate math courses.

This technique will work whether you study by yourself or in a group. The advantage to working in a group is that groups of people are less likely to miss something important than one individual. The advantage to working by yourself is that you can set your own pace and schedule. The key, once again, is to practice. Writing down the important formulas and representative problems is a form of practice. When you condense the list and condense it again, you are rehearsing for the test.

Portions of many courses are like mathematics in that they require practice. In physics, much of what you do is solving equations. In chemistry, some of your time is spent balancing reactions. In symbolic logic, your major task is building proofs. In speech, you must give speeches. And so on. In all of these courses, practice is crucial. The same techniques I have been recommending for math courses will work for them.

EXERCISE 10.1

In your journal, write about your homework for your math (or physics, or accounting, or symbolic logic) course. What makes Problem 3 hard? What makes Problem 5 easier for you? How did you go about solving Problem 3? Write down each step, no matter how trivial. What do you suppose your instructor wants you to learn from this assignment? What did you learn from it? What's likely to be on the test?

What you are doing with this exercise is creating a study log. Study logs give you a way to reflect on your homework. They are extremely valuable. They force you to actually think about what you are studying; when you think about it, you learn it. You may find study logs helpful in all of your courses.

Accounting Courses

In accounting courses you must both understand the theory and be able to solve problems. If you can only do one or the other, you're in trouble.

The first few weeks of most accounting courses are devoted to the structure of a complete bookkeeping system. You must understand how the complete system works in order to succeed in the course. Read your text very slowly, concentrate hard, and use your pencil—just as you do with a math text. Take it section by section. Pay close attention to the diagrams and samples. Work out the examples with your pencil. Do all of the exercises provided, and ask for more if you think you need additional practice.

Accounting, like math, is cumulative. If you don't understand Chapter 2, you'll be lost in Chapter 3. If you don't understand the early portions of the course—if you don't have a grasp of how the overall accounting system works—you'll be helpless before long. For instance, there are several methods for calculating depreciation. The ultimate aim is to maximize net income; the task is to figure out which method of depreciation will yield the highest income. In order to reach a conclusion, you can't simply plug numbers into a formula; you must understand how the entire system works.

Writing Courses

Most colleges require students (usually freshmen) to take one or two composition courses. Many also require some writing-intensive courses (courses that include several papers, essay tests, or significant amounts of some other sort of writing) beyond the composition requirement. Writing courses, like math and accounting courses, require performance. If you don't write well, you don't do well.

Writing, like math, is a skill that can be learned. In order to learn it, you must practice. Your composition instructor will give you lots of things to write: a journal, paragraphs describing your roommate or spouse, short in-class essays, take-home papers, research papers, and so on. And he will give you lots of good advice: Start your papers as soon as you receive the assignment; talk the topic over with someone; write a draft and show it to someone; rewrite, and rewrite again before you turn it in.

Unfortunately, many students ignore that advice. They begin their papers the night before they are due, scramble around for a topic, scribble a draft, and turn it in. When they get poor grades, they say they "just can't write." Baloney. They just *didn't* write.

In order to write well, you must practice. Do the things your composition instructor tells you to do—and more. Any time you are putting words on paper (or on screen with a word processor), you are writing. Letters home, notes to your housemate, entries in your journal, and answers to essay questions all count as practice writing. They won't suffice to make you a good writer, but they will help. And if you can get some helpful feedback about some of your writing—the first draft of your paper, for instance—you can make swift and visible progress.

Think about writing whenever you practice. Notice the words you use and why you use them. Pay attention to tense, to case, and to parallelism. The more conscious you can become of the elements of good writing as you practice, the more effective that practice will be when you must perform. And pay attention to the way others write. Look at the word choice, the sentence construction, and the format in your texts, in the newspaper, in the letters you get from home. As you become more aware of the techniques of writing, you can learn from the way other writers use those techniques.

Fortunately for all of us, writing has recently become much easier than it once was. The development of inexpensive personal computers and word-processing software has been an enormous benefit. Writers used to have to retype or rescribble their work every time they wanted to revise. Nowadays you just make whatever changes you like in your electronic file and print a new copy. Rewriting, once torturous, is quite pleasant. Seeing your very own words scroll down the screen and changing them with just a few keystrokes is exhilarating.

Word processors have eliminated or reduced many of the psychological blocks facing writers. The blank page syndrome—being paralyzed by the blank page—has virtually disappeared. Staring at a blank screen can be paralyzing also, but blank screens are easily filled in. Type in the assignment, and stare at that instead of the blank screen. Add the key concepts you have already thought of, begin listing some of the things you want to say, jot down the conclusion you wish to reach, and you'll have a lot to stare at, think about, and write. When you've finished your paper, go back and erase the extra stuff at the beginning.

Many students say that they could write their papers "if they just had a start." With a word processor, you can invent as many beginnings as you like and see how they work. Or you can start in the middle, at the end, or anywhere you have something to say. Before long, your beginning will come to you, and you can add it.

Writer's block is easier to get over than it used to be. When you are blocked, write anything: List key words, restate the conclusion you want to draw, brainstorm by writing anything that comes to your mind. Sooner or later, words you want to use will appear on your screen, and the block will be broken.

In short, word processors make it easier to practice your writing. Use one. If you don't have one of your own, or if you don't have access to your roommate's or your dad's computer, use the computer lab at school. Virtually all colleges provide some sort of computer facility for their students. Check it out, and take advantage of it.

Foreign Language Courses

Foreign language courses are very much like mathematics courses. In order to succeed in a foreign language course you must perform: You must be able to translate, to handle the grammar, to pronounce, and so on. In order to be able to perform adequately, you must practice.

Your instructor knows that. Consequently, he will give you lots of opportunities to practice in class and lots of drills to do at home. Take them seriously. Too many students treat the various exercises their French or Swahili professors give them as busy work, as not worthy of their attention. Too few students think of them as practice for the big performance: the exam.

All of the techniques recommended for math courses work for foreign language courses. Doing your homework is the best way to practice; take it seriously. While you are doing it, reflect: Why is this sentence structured this way? Why is she asking me to learn the passive voice? If the past tense of *this* verb is so-and-so, what's the past tense of *that* verb? And so on. Expand on your homework, too. If your French assignment is to name all of the objects you can see without turning your head, do it. Then turn your head and do it again. The more practice you get, the better.

Just like math and accounting courses, foreign language courses are cumulative: What you learn tomorrow will depend on what you learn today. You must keep up. With other courses you can sometimes get away with putting off a reading assignment for a while, but not in a foreign language course. Study groups are good ways to keep up. They serve as a conscience as well as a medium for learning what you need to learn.

Practice tests are extremely helpful. Your instructor can probably supply some for you. Better yet, get together with one or more colleagues and invent your own. Once again, reflect on the practice test after you complete it: What did you handle easily and what gave you trouble? What should you work on before the exam? Are these questions likely to appear on the test? Do some writing before the exam as well: crucial vocabulary, verb declensions, accent marks, and so on.

► EXERCISE 10.2 ◄

In preparation for your next exam in the foreign language you are studying, prepare a crib sheet. Write down everything you think might be on the test: vocabulary, grammatical rules, sample paragraphs for translation, potential essay questions, and so forth. Now condense everything you've written onto one sheet. Include only the most important vocabulary words or words that represent classes of words; the most significant, most general grammatical rules; one or two tricks that will help you translate anything ("watch for subjunctives, remember accent marks"); and the most likely topics for essay questions. You may have to write very small and use every bit of space.

Now carry this sheet around with you. Review it while you're standing in line for lunch, while you're waiting for class, or during your study breaks. Just before the exam, throw it away. You'd never get away with using it during the test, right? Besides, if you've followed these steps—writing twice and reviewing a lot—you don't need it anymore.

There are hundreds of ways to practice a foreign language. While you're reading the newpaper, translate as many of the words as you can into Spanish. Make up German captions for the pictures in *People* or *Sports Illustrated.* Try to read a Japanese comic book. Speak French with the foreign exchange student down the hall or Spanish when you go to Mexico on vacation. Write a lab report in Arabic, a paragraph of a political science paper in Norwegian, or an entry in your journal in Polish. You use English constantly; whenever you use English, you can use the language you are studying instead. That's practice.

Outside-of-Class Activities

Band, choir, theater, and athletics are all performance-oriented activities. If you are seriously involved in any of them—that is, involved beyond the level of playing in a pick-up band or intramural sports—you must practice in order to be able to perform. You must practice regularly, you must concentrate on what you're doing, you must reflect on what you have done so you can do it again next time, and you must persist.

How can you do that and succeed in your courses? Well, it's hard sometimes, but lots of students do it. First of all, you must have a clear set of priorities (see Chapter 1). Second, you must schedule your time carefully, in accord with those priorities (see Chapter 2). Finally, you must integrate your coursework and your out-of-class activities as much as you possibly can (see Chapter 4).

Use the same techniques for practicing basketball and statistics, for practicing the saxophone and accounting, for practicing your part for the play and your verbs for French. In basketball, your coach teaches you a specific technique for playing defense. In practice, you apply that technique against all sorts of offenses, in all sorts of situations. In statistics, your instructor and your text teach you a method for finding the standard deviation. In your practice—in working your homework problems—you apply that method to all sorts of statistical problems, in all sorts of situations.

In basketball, it helps to think about what you are doing while you do it: What happens if I jump out more quickly? What if we *don't* switch? You should think about your statistics while you are doing it as well: What happens if the curve has a slightly different shape? What if the sample is larger? In both basketball and statistics, reflecting on what you have learned is enormously valuable. Why does coach want you to play this defense? How does it fit into her overall philosophy of the game? Why are you doing standard deviations? When would you use them in your chosen profession?

You might even find ways to combine your study of basketball and your study of statistics. By computing the shooting percentages of the starting five from within and outside the three-point line, you will both give your coach a good analytical tool for figuring who should shoot from where and practice your statistics.

EXERCISE 10.3

In working through this book, you have practiced many of the techniques you have read about. It's time to reflect on that practice. Read through the journal entries you have made so far. Now write for 10 minutes on what you have learned so far. Finally, address these questions in your journal: Did you learn best by simply reading or did practicing in your journal help? Which of the various tricks you have learned have helped you already? How will you ensure that you keep using them? If you had to take an exam on this book next week, how would you study for it?

Summary

Many of your courses and activities will require you to perform. It isn't enough simply to understand the concepts; you must put the concepts to work. In order to perform in these courses, you must practice. To practice effectively you must use a particular technique or method in a variety of situations. You must reflect on what you have just done so you can remember it. And you must integrate your knowledge of the technique or method with the rest of your knowledge base so you can use it again in new and different situations.

Putting It All Together

So far we have been working mostly in the abstract. Let's conclude by bringing the abstract lessons you have learned to bear on some specific cases. Jason and Connie, whose stories appear in Chapter 11, are both bound for professions. Melissa and Claude, from Chapter 12, are primarily interested in the content of their coursework. Alex and Leandra, Chapter 13, like to party; Aaron and Suzy, Chapter 14, are athletes. These stories demonstrate how the principles of succeeding in college from Part I and the techniques of succeeding in college from Part II can actually make a difference. **T**he eight students whose stories make up Part III are composites of students I have known over the years. They are not actual individuals, but they are real.

11

The Preprofessionals

Many, perhaps most, students come to college with a fairly definite notion of the profession they will enter. Sometimes they continue on the path they originally charted; other times they veer in another direction. Few courses are smooth.

Jason

Jason is a new freshman this fall. He was a hero in high school: athlete (second-team all-conference defensive back), president of student council, king of the homecoming court. He was a good student, but not wonderful. He earned a few As, a few Cs, and lots of Bs. His folks made him take both the SAT and the ACT, and his scores were in the 70th percentile range. Everybody loved him.

He applied to and was accepted by three colleges: the state university, the local branch of the state college system, and a small liberal arts college 100 miles away. The liberal arts college offered him a healthy financial aid package—they loved him too—and the chance to keep playing football, so he accepted their offer. In early September his folks drove him to campus, helped him register, kissed him goodbye, and left.

Football went fine. Classes did not. In high school, Jason didn't have much time for studying. Late afternoons were for football, wrestling, and baseball. The job at Burger World took up an evening or two and most weekends. His girlfriend took most of the rest. He did most of his homework, but in the shortest possible time. He seldom read his textbooks, but studied hard for tests. His native intelligence, quick wit, and general lovableness earned him his good-enough grades.

Without thinking much about it, Jason followed the same pattern in college. He went to class and listened, but didn't take notes—in high school, notebooks were for losers. He did his assignments in Calculus because the instructor checked them. But he ignored most of the reading assignments in World History, Psychology, and English Composition. Not much time, with practice and all; besides, the instructors never seemed to mention them in class. He knew he was just as smart as he ever was, and just as lovable. Why shouldn't he continue to succeed?

He studied hard for his first math exam and earned a B. But the English paper he whipped off the hour before it was due came back with a D− and "SEE ME" written in red across the top. Before he got around to seeing his English instructor—football trip, and besides, who wants to get yelled at?—he took exams in psych and history. He closeted himself in his room the night before the tests and studied a solid 5 hours for each. The results: F and C−.

The folks were displeased, coach was angry, and Jason was confused. He was working hard, by his standards. He was starting on the jayvees and playing a little with the varsity. Everybody liked him. Why wasn't he earning better grades? His coach sent him to the freshman adviser in the Counseling Center.

The adviser pointed out the obvious. "You're not taking notes. You're not reading your assignments. You're not starting your English papers far enough in advance, and you're not rewriting them. You're putting off your preparation for tests too long." And the adviser prescribed some remedies.

"Take notes; the junior and senior football players do. At least skim your assignments; I'll show you how. Go see your English instructor. Start your papers the day they are assigned by jotting an outline in your notebook. Write a rough draft 2 days before each paper is due, have someone critique it for you, and *then* type the final draft. Start studying for big exams the week before, not the night before."

Jason took as much of this advice as he could stomach. He took some notes during class, without knowing what to write down or what to do with them afterwards. He skimmed some of his assignments. He saw his English instructor, who explained that his first paper wasn't bad but failed to address the assigned topic. He got the next topic straight and wrote a rough draft but then typed it verbatim. And 2 nights before his second psych exam he began to review his notes and the reading he had skimmed.

It helped; he got a C on the psych exam and a B− on his English paper. But doing all that stuff took much of the time he had been spending on his math assignments, so he stopped doing them. And even though he started studying for the math test 3 whole days beforehand he didn't quite understand the basic concepts, and he failed it. More unhappy phone calls with the folks, more yelling from coach, more confusion.

Jason met with his adviser again. This time they went beyond the obvious. "Why are you going to college?" he asked. Jason was startled; no one had ever asked him that before. "Because everybody goes to college, I guess. You need a degree to get a good job; that's why I plan to major in business. My folks always expected me to go."

The adviser led Jason through a goal-setting exercise similar to the one in Chapter 1. Jason's ultimate aim was to be a prosperous father; to get there he intended to graduate with at least a 3.3 GPA, complete a master's degree in business administration, and work for a large corporation. An interest inventory and an aptitude test confirmed that he was well suited for a business career. Jason agreed that the grades he was currently earning would not allow him to reach his goals and that he would have to change his study patterns.

The next day they charted Jason's daily schedule. It turned out that Jason was wasting three or four prime study hours when he didn't have class during the day. The adviser told him to spend those hours in the library reading his assignments, doing his math homework, working on his papers, and preparing for tests.

"But what if I don't have any homework?" Jason asked. "Stop thinking in terms of homework," answered the adviser. "Think in terms of learning what you need to know to achieve your goals. In football, what happens if all you do is your assignment—cover the wide receiver or whatever?"

"Not much happens if all I do is my assignment. I try to watch the whole play, figure out what the quarterback is planning, and then go for the ball. If all I do is watch the wide receiver, I'm at his mercy; all I can do is react."

"Right. It's like that in college, too. You should be doing more than just reacting; you should figure out what you need to do to get where you want to be. For instance, you need to learn how to do calculus. It's required for business, and you should earn at least a B to keep your

GPA up. Doing your homework is only part of learning calculus. You should also be taking practice tests, studying with a study group, asking your instructor about the problems you just can't figure out. Don't think about just doing your homework; think about achieving your goals.

"You need Bs and Cs in your other courses to build a solid GPA, right? And you want to keep your folks and the coach off your back. What do you have to learn to make those grades?"

"Well, in psych I have to be able to define a bunch of terms on the test. And I have to know what lots of famous psychologists—Freud, Jung, and them—had to say. My history prof gives nothing but essay tests, so I have to be able to write about the causes of historical events: the rise of Greece, the fall of Rome, and so on. To write good answers I have to know what happened and why. In English I have to learn how to write good papers, I guess."

"Let's take psych first. You can earn at least a C if you get Bs on the remaining three tests. Now, how do you learn what the terms mean? How do you learn what those psychologists said?"

"Well, it's all in the book. And the instructor goes over some of it in class, but not everything that's in the book. I guess he lectures about the terms and psychologists he thinks are the most important; he's never tested us on stuff that wasn't in the lecture."

"So one way to get the grades you want on the tests is to listen to the lectures, write down the terms and their definitions, the psychologists and what they said, in your notebook. Then read the parts of the book that were summarized in the lecture. You could do your reading during that free hour right after psych class, when it's all fresh in your mind."

"But aren't we supposed to do the reading before the lecture?" Jason asked.

"Skim the reading before the lecture so you have some idea of what's coming up. But if he only tests on parts of the reading assignments, there's no point in spending lots of time reading the rest. A few days before the exam, get together with two or three other people and review your definitions. Make up practice questions for each other. Summarize the beliefs of Freud and Jung. You'll find that an hour spent reviewing with others is worth 3 hours studying by yourself."

They followed a similar process for all of his courses. In history, they agreed that Jason needed to earn Bs. To do that, he had to read his text quite thoroughly because the instructor took at least a few questions on each test from the book. He also had to pay close attention in class and take good notes. The lectures were well-organized descriptions of the causes of historical events. The adviser showed Jason how to take notes as well organized as the lectures: Write on one side only, new thoughts get new paragraphs, review your notes nightly, take notes-on-your-notes, and so forth.

Jason's English instructor had told him during their conference that his basic writing skills were sound but that he needed to pay more attention to assignments. And he had to rewrite, rewrite, rewrite. The adviser told Jason to visit the college Writing Center as soon as an assignment for an English paper was made. The peer tutors there would help him figure out the assignment and write an outline, and they would schedule an appointment to review his draft—at least 2 days before the paper was due. With good preparation, they agreed that As were definitely within reach. And an A in English composition would serve him well in business.

By the end of the quarter Jason was earning Bs and an A in English. His folks were relieved, coach was silent, and he was proud of himself.

What happened here? Why did Jason struggle early and succeed later? First, Jason had very little idea why he was going to college. He had always assumed that he would go, and so he did. But that sort of assumption does not provide very much motivation when the going gets tough. When he began to figure out why he was in college, he could begin to see the reasons for doing the work he was asked to do, and so he began to do it.

Second, Jason had been very successful in high school without doing very much studying. Consequently he didn't know how to read a text, take notes, handle a paper assignment, or prepare for a test. In high school, being smart and athletic and lovable was enough. In college, it wasn't. Once he began to study seriously, he began to succeed.

Third, Jason thought of school as a place where people did things to you. Teachers stuff information in your head through lectures and textbooks and then give you a test to see how much you remember. As long as you do most of what they tell you to do and smile, you're okay. But in college that strategy didn't work. His instructors didn't care much if he smiled, and doing most of what they told him to do wasn't nearly enough.

More work is required, true. But a different attitude is required as well. Succeeding in college is a matter of deciding what you want to get out of it and then doing whatever has to be done to reach your goal. Jason finally began to understand that after meeting with the freshman adviser. From that point on, college became a place where he could control his own destiny—not where people did things to him.

Connie

Connie is a 33-year-old legal secretary. She graduated from high school 15 years ago, worked for 5 years in a law office, married an attorney, and had two children. She was recently divorced. She receives child support but must work at least part time to support herself and her family. This year, with the help of a friendly admissions counselor, she enrolled in the community college in her town. She is studying to be a paralegal; her aim is to make herself more employable.

Connie was a good student in high school, but she took few college preparatory courses. Her mathematics skills were seriously deficient. She struggled through Business Math and never attempted algebra. The paralegal program requires a semester of algebra; that terrified her.

The admissions counselor assured her that the Help Center could give her as much assistance as she needs. "We see hundreds of women returning to school," she said. "Many of them have no math skills, so we're used to helping. Go to the Help Center on the first day of class." She did; unfortunately, so did dozens of other students, all younger than Connie. She decided that she could learn algebra on her own.

Her instructor was a graduate student at the local university supplementing her assistantship by teaching in the community college. Fortunately for Connie, she was sympathetic to her students' travails. Still, the course was designed to teach a year of high school algebra in one semester. Students who had not studied math for some time, like Connie, got into serious difficulty very quickly. The instructor did her best to help during her limited office hours, but frequently the best she could do was refer students to the still-crowded Help Center.

By the sixth week in the semester, Connie was ready to drop out of college. Her other courses were going well enough. English I was no problem, though a little boring; her first paper earned a C++, and she was receiving 8s and 9s on the weekly 10-point quizzes. Concepts of Law, the introductory course for paralegals, was a snap. The text was easy to read, the tests came directly from the book, and so she was carrying a solid A. (The only hard part was keeping silent when the instructor described how the law works; in her experience, the instructor's tales had nothing to do with reality.) Political Science, her elective, was demanding, but she was managing to earn Cs.

Math, however, was a disaster area. She was spending a lot of time on her math homework and getting credit for most of it. But she could not pass the tests. She understood the basic concepts, she thought: X stands for an unknown, and the point is to manipulate what is known to find out what X is. Her difficulty lay in manipulating the numbers. On the homework, she could look at the way similar problems were solved in the text and use the same techniques. But on the tests, there were no models to follow; consequently she became hopelessly confused and failed.

The math course was required for her program, and she couldn't pass the math course; didn't that prove that she was just not smart enough for college? That's what her ex-husband had told her, after all. What could she do but drop out? The law firm would be happy to have her work full time. Even if the money was lousy, she could make do. And her children needed her.

The friendly admissions counselor was aghast. "You're only doing poorly in one course. And you enjoy the rest, so why should you let that one course screw up your plans for your life?" "Because," said Connie, "if I fail that one course I can't be a paralegal at all; it's required. Besides, if I can't do algebra, that shows I'm just stupid."

The counselor suggested that Connie drop the math course instead of dropping out of school altogether. She could use some of the time she used to spend on her algebra homework on her other courses and the rest working on math in the Help Center. "The Help Center's always crowded," Connie replied. "And I don't fit in—they're all kids."

"It's not nearly as crowded now as it was the first day; most of those students were signing up for the tutoring program. And what do you care if it's all kids? You're a student here too. In fact, you have more potential than most of those kids. I just love admitting students like you; your chances at succeeding here, or at any other college, are much better than those of most of the 18-year-olds who make you so nervous. For two reasons: You know how to work and they don't, and you know what the alternatives are. If you can't become a paralegal, or even a lawyer, you're going to be stuck as a secretary the rest of your life—and you know what that's like. So you're going to work as hard as you can to avoid that fate. The 18-year-olds think they're going to live forever and be able to do whatever they want, so they have no fate to avoid. And the only jobs they've ever had are part-time or summer work; they don't know much about working hard."

"But if I drop algebra, won't I be behind everyone else? And I still have to take it some day."

"You can take it next semester, or the semester after that. The program doesn't care, as long as you pass. In the meantime you can figure out why it's so hard for you."

So Connie dropped her math course and went back to the Help Center. They gave her a battery of diagnostic tests and discovered that her basic arithmetic skills were weak. She could add, subtract, and multiply, but dividing was hard. And dividing fractions was next to impossible. Without arithmetic, they told her, you can't do algebra.

She began an individualized arithmetic program. She met with one of the Help Center staff now and again, but she spent most of her time working through the texts and computer programs they assigned her. By the end of the semester she was dividing fractions in her head.

Her other courses improved as well. Her English papers got better as she caught on to the requirements of academic writing: A−. Concepts of Law continued to be easy and irrelevant: A. Political Science was harder. The instructor required class discussion—tough for Connie, the oldest in the class—and gave essay tests. But by the end of the quarter she was speaking at least once each meeting, and everyone listened. Essay questions, she figured out, are not just requests for information; they're prompts for arguments. If she treated them like the sorts of challenges she used to hear from her fellow workers around the lunch table, she could produce an argument that made sense. Final grade: B+.

Second semester, Connie reenrolled in algebra. And she began to think about law school.

Connie turned out to be a very successful student. What held her back as a new freshman? Her biggest obstacle was her helplessness in math. College courses assume that you have certain basic academic skills: You must know arithmetic (and, in many institutions, algebra); you must be able to read and write, at least at the ninth- or tenth-grade level; you must be able to speak coherently; and so on. If you cannot, you will have difficulty, as Connie did.

But, as Connie found, even if you lack one or more of these basic skills, all is not lost. Colleges have learned—the hard way—that many of the people they want to admit lack some of these skills. And so most colleges have created something like the Help Center where Connie learned her arithmetic. They are called a variety of names— Academic Skills Center, Basic Skills Office, Tutoring Office, Remediation, Inc., Developmental Ed—and they are housed everywhere from the library to the World War II quonset hut beyond the field house. But they are there, and they are devoted to helping you learn whatever you must learn to be ready for your classes.

Connie also suffered from a lack of confidence, as do many older students. They have been out of school for so long it all seems foreign to them; they don't know how to dress, talk, or act. The 18-year-olds know how to dress, talk, and act, and so they seem smarter. Well, they're not. As soon as Connie began to see that she could compete, she began to succeed.

Further, older students (or nontraditionals, or returning adults; different institutions have different euphemisms) bring a wealth of experience to class with them. That experience gives them a tremendous advantage over the 18-year-olds. Connie's years of lunchtime conversations gave her the tools to answer essay questions; her younger colleagues did not have that experience.

Finally, Connie did not understand that college is a place in which you can set your own goals and go after them in your own way. Like Jason, she thought that school was a place in which the students followed the rules or else they didn't succeed. If she couldn't pass algebra, she couldn't become a paralegal. Her friend the admissions counselor helped her understand that college is a system of rules, true, but that the system is meant to be worked to the students' advantage. If she couldn't pass algebra, she should back up a step, develop her math skills, and try again; the system didn't want her to give up. And once Connie began to take control of her education, she began to succeed—just as Jason did.

Jason and Connie are very different individuals. The problems they faced are different, and the solutions they found are different. But note that there are a few common elements.

First, both Jason and Connie found some help when they needed it. They found it in different places, from different sorts of people. Jason went to the freshman adviser in the Counseling Center and found both a sympathetic ear and good advice. Connie returned to the admissions counselor who had admitted her to college for assistance. And they got very different sorts of help. Jason needed to set his goals and learn some specific study techniques; Connie needed reassurance and to learn arithmetic. But both saw that they were in trouble and found someone who could help.

Does that mean that someone in the Counseling Center or the Admissions Office can solve all your problems for you? Not at all. The second common element in these two cases is that Jason and Connie learned from and used the advice they received. They changed their ways of thinking and changed their behavior accordingly. In other words, it's not enough to know that you are in trouble or even to know what your trouble is. You have to do something about it.

Which of these two students, Jason or Connie, do you admire the most? Why? Have you faced, or do you face, any of the same difficulties? What did you, or will you, do about them? Write your answers in your journal.

12

The Scholars

Some students are driven by an interest in their coursework. They like the intellectual challenge of learning. They enjoy thinking and talking and writing about ideas. School is easy for them, right? Not always.

Melissa

Melissa was almost a straight-A student in high school. She worked hard, did all of her homework exactly as her teachers told her, memorized lists and formulas and dates and names for days before exams, and graduated near the top of her class. She came to the State University this fall to become an elementary school teacher.

At midsemester she went home for a visit. "It's not the same as high school, Mom," she said. "I can't figure out what I'm supposed to know. So far I've gotten Cs in philosophy and English and a B− in biology; I don't know what to do."

Her mother had never gone to college. The best advice she could give was to hang in there and see if things got better by Christmas break. If they didn't, maybe Melissa should think about going to the local tech school to become a licensed practical nurse.

On her return to campus, Melissa found she had received a C− on an English paper—the one she had stayed up late 3 nights for, the one she had rewritten six times, the one she was positive was absolutely perfect. She went to see her English instructor.

"Dr. Johnson, I just don't understand this grade. You found only one mistake, a nonparallel construction, and you gave me a C−! I worked really hard on this paper—here are all my drafts—and I thought it was perfect. And it was almost perfect; only one mistake! What do I have to do to get an A?"

"Melissa, it's true that your paper had only one grammatical mistake. But look at the comment I wrote at the end: 'This paper is mechanically sound, but it says nothing. The assignment was to write a descriptive paper on the topic, What does Gulliver look like through the eyes of a Lilliputian? You wrote a summary of *Gulliver's Travels*.' Now, your summary was accurate enough, but it didn't have much to do with the assignment. That's why you got a C−. Actually, I almost gave you a D. But it was clear that you had worked hard and long on your summary, so I gave you the benefit of the doubt. But you really have to do better than this, Melissa."

Melissa broke into tears, wailing about how unfair college was. In high school she could just repeat what the teacher said on tests and papers and make automatic As. In college she didn't know what she was supposed to write.

Dr. Johnson gave her a tissue and asked her to say more about her high school days. Was she ever asked to use her imagination? Did she ever write any fantasy papers or do any brainstorming? Did she work on the school newspaper or the yearbook? Melissa had done none of those things; she was too busy doing her homework and memorizing things for tests.

Melissa's difficulty, Dr. Johnson found, was that she had never had to do any thinking in high school. She had structured her courses and activities so that she could always succeed by simply following directions. But some of her college courses required her to think. Her philosophy instructor kept asking her "What's wrong with this argument?" or "Why did this philosopher make that claim?" She didn't know! And she was offended by the question. It was the instructor's job to explain those things, not the student's.

"And in English," Melissa explained, "the paper assignments are all so weird. Who cares what Gulliver looked like through a Lilliputian's eyes? The point of reading *Gulliver's Travels* is to find out what it said, right? And to figure out how he said it—Swift's use of metaphor and all that. Why should we have to imagine weird stuff, like how he looked through someone else's eyes?"

"Because imagining how a normal-sized person looks through the eyes of an extremely small creature stretches your imagination. The point of Freshman English is to help you learn to use language in a variety of ways; describing weird stuff is one."

By this time Melissa figured she had ruined her entire college career by speaking so boldly. The tech school was looking better every minute, and nursing would be okay. "But why do I need that stuff? I'm not an English major, I'm in Elementary Education. I don't plan on writing anything ever again after I get out of this course—which may never happen, if I can't get better than a C−."

Dr. Johnson explained to Melissa that she would be writing things for the rest of her life: lesson plans, program proposals, grant applications, yearly reports, letters, notes home to parents, and so on. Indeed, the Elementary Education program at the State University had recently added a writing requirement for admission into the major. Melissa would have to pass a special writing test by the beginning of her junior year.

But there were even more important reasons for doing all this weird stuff, as Dr. Johnson pointed out to Melissa. "First of all, it's fun. If you let your imagination go a little, you can have a great time imagining what a giant Gulliver must have seemed. Think of what his fingers and toes looked like! Secondly, doing these thought experiments helps you think. By imagining what Gulliver looked like, you begin to see the world in a different perspective. And that will help you realize that your own perspective is not always the only one."

"My philosophy instructor told us almost the same thing the other day: 'The only way to understand Plato's argument fully is to see the world through his eyes.' I understand that, I guess. But I still don't see why I should understand Plato's argument or the Lilliputians' point of view either. I'm going to be a grade school teacher, if I can ever get through college. Teachers don't have to understand all that weird stuff. They just have to know arithmetic and geography and how to tie shoes."

"Let me ask you this, Melissa: Do you think you might be a better teacher if you can see arithmetic and geography and shoelaces through the eyes of a 6-year-old?"

Well, Melissa got the point. And she began to see that her English and philosophy courses were teaching her some basic thinking skills that she would need as a teacher. She and Dr. Johnson had frequent conversations during the rest of the semester and met occasionally for the next few years. (Dr. Johnson saw a little of herself in Melissa; she had been something of a mindless perfectionist in high school also.)

And Melissa began to use her imagination in her English papers and in the discussions in her philosophy class. Dr. Johnson showed her that free-writing in her journal could help stimulate her creativity. She liked it; she could write *anything*, and what she wrote frequently led her into new ways of thinking, writing, and speaking. She found too that writing in her journal helped her process the information she was gathering in her other classes. Before long she was memorizing less and learning more.

Her grades slowly improved to Bs and As, she passed the writing test for education majors, and she was admitted to the Elementary Education program. But during the summer before her junior year she decided that she might want to be a college teacher instead, so she changed her major to English.

Melissa was a victim of her own success, in a way. She learned early in her grade school career that the way to succeed was to follow directions: Color between the lines, walk on the right, and so on. She followed directions very well and got very good grades. In high school she avoided the courses and instructors and activities that might have required something other than following directions, so she continued to earn very good grades.

But in college it didn't work. (Actually it worked to some degree in some courses. She earned a B+ in Introduction to Biology by memorizing before tests, just as she had in high school. But she was frustrated by the A her roommate received in the same course by doing half the work.) Her English and philosophy courses required some thinking, some imagination; she had never used those skills in school before. As soon as Dr. Johnson convinced her that imagination and creativity were legitimate academic tools, Melissa began to succeed again.

Claude

Claude was the weird guy in high school. He earned As in the classes he liked and Ds in the rest. He liked physics; it was easy to relate it to the science fiction he'd been reading since third grade. He liked photography; creating things in the darkroom was neat. He hated any class that required working with other people: chemistry, where he had to work with a lab partner; English, where the instructor made everyone give 5-minute talks; physical education, where everything was team sports. Some history was okay. Reading about other times and other places was neat.

Claude registered at the mega-university in his state as a physics major. He told everyone he would be a physicist, but deep down inside he wanted to become a famous science fiction writer. He enrolled in Physics I, Freshman Composition, History of Western Civilization, Calculus I, and Orientation to College (a one-credit course for students with mediocre high school grades).

He hated it. Freshman Composition was even worse than high school English. The instructor insisted that everyone keep journals, and then she read them. Sometimes she read passages aloud. Western Civilization was not bad; the reading was interesting, and the professor gave good lectures. But every now and then he insisted that the class break into small groups to discuss something, and Claude hated that. Calculus was math—Claude could always do math. Orientation to College was a bore. The instructor, who insisted on being called the facilitator, just sat around talking about reading and study skills techniques.

Physics was the worst. First of all, he had to work with three lab partners. They were all more aggressive than Claude, so they tended to take over the experiment—even though Claude had read more physics than any of them! Second, the kind of physics Claude was interested in wasn't even on the syllabus. When he asked the professor, she said that they wouldn't get to quantum mechanics until Physics II. "You can't run till you walk," she said. "Master Newtonian mechanics first; then you'll be ready for Einstein and Bohr."

Claude decided in his second week that Physics was not for him, so he stopped going to class. He got a B— on his first paper in Freshman Composition; all that reading paid off. He immersed himself in Western Civilization, reading everything that was assigned, everything that was suggested, and everything that the instructor mentioned in passing. He endured the small group discussions for a while, and then found that no one objected if he just walked out of class when they began. He received the highest A in the class on the first exam but missed two quizzes.

Orientation to College seemed to have nothing to teach him at all. He stopped going to that also. Calculus was still math; he rather enjoyed the mental challenge of working the problems and earned solid Bs.

Unfortunately, Claude missed the session in Orientation to College devoted to the university's academic policies. He never learned that when you stop going to class you still appear on the roll—that no one can drop you from the course but you. At midsemester his adviser received a notice that Claude was failing Physics and Orientation to College. He dutifully placed the notice in Claude's file, intending to speak to him about it at their next scheduled meeting. But Claude had already forgotten who his adviser was, and so they never met.

At semester's end Claude earned a B— in Calculus, an Incomplete in Freshman Composition, an A— in History of Western Civilization, and Fs in Physics and Orientation to College. His grades were just good enough to keep him in good standing, but the dean sent him a note encouraging him to see his adviser immediately. He ignored it.

Second semester, Claude took Freshman Composition II, History of Ancient Greece, Classic Science Fiction, and Fencing. He couldn't avoid composition; all second-semester freshmen had to take it. History of Ancient Greece sounded wonderful, and he had done so well in History of Western Civilization; why not try it again? Science Fiction was his dream, and he'd always wanted to try fencing.

His choices turned out poorly. He had the same instructor for composition, and she kept asking him when he was going to write the three papers he owed her from Freshman Composition I. His history professor was dry as dust—nothing like first semester. The science fiction course was taught by an ancient professor of English literature who thought that science fiction ended with H. G. Wells. Fencing was okay, but it would be more fun if the foils didn't have those little balls on the end.

Claude lasted until midsemester. By then he had failed exams in two classes, failed to turn in three papers in composition, and cut himself three times with a saber. He had stopped going to all of his classes but fencing. He went home. At semester's end he received all Fs, and he was notified that he was on academic probation for the following year. He never read the notice.

What happened here? Why did Claude, a bright student interested in several academic disciplines, fail in college? For several reasons. First, his goals were not very clearly defined, even in his own mind. He had an itch to be a famous science fiction writer, but he could not even bring himself to articulate his itch to himself, let alone to another person. Consequently, his goal had little to do with the courses he took or the way he attacked them.

Secondly, he absolutely refused to work with anyone else. He ignored his adviser; he shunned his Orientation to College class; he spent no time with his roommate or any classmates; he dropped physics in part to avoid working with lab partners. He relied entirely on his own resources, his own knowledge, his own experiences—and they did not serve him well.

Third, he ignored the structure and the policies of the university. He came to college with a naive view that undergraduates could just take the courses they were interested in, learn what they wanted to know, and then get a degree. But it doesn't work that way. Colleges and universities are extremely complicated bureaucratic structures. In order to succeed in them, students must learn how they work and to use university policies to their own advantage. Claude paid no attention.

Fourth, he refused all offers of assistance. His History of Western Civilization professor was rather taken with Claude and offered to befriend him. Claude wasn't interested. Two of the guys in his residence hall wanted him to join their Calculus study group; Claude refused. His instructor for Orientation to College asked him to come see her; Claude declined. She eventually sent his name to the Counseling Center as a student at risk. Claude resisted their overtures as well.

Claude came to college with a set of beliefs and ideas that led him astray. So did Jason and Connie and Melissa. But they saw the errors of their ways of thinking and did something about it. Claude did not.

Is Claude doomed? Not at all. He is at home, reading science fiction and working at the library. The head librarian talks to him a lot, and he sometimes responds. She is urging him to try college again. He might.

Melissa succeeded by infusing some imagination and creativity into her academic life. Does that mean that imagination and creativity are all you need to succeed in college? Certainly not. Look at Claude. He was both creative and imaginative, but he was terribly undisciplined, refused to work with anyone else, and ignored the rules of the institution he was enrolled in.

The major difference between them is that Melissa found a way around her initial failure and pursued it. Claude did not, at least while he was still enrolled. He may still.

EXERCISE 12.1

Two thought experiments: Write your answers in your journal.

1. Imagine that you are Claude's older brother or sister, visiting him during fall semester. What do you tell him? How do you help him?
2. Imagine Claude and Melissa meeting while waiting in line to register for second semester. They like each other. What do they say?

CHAPTER 13

The Fun Seekers

Some students come to college searching for fun. That's not their only reason, to be sure—they know that they'll need to go to work eventually, they know that they'll need that degree. But having a good time comes first on their lists of goals.

Alex

Alex hustled his way through high school. He did some of the work, of course, and occasionally did it very well. But he frequently managed to find an alternative to the assignment: writing a paper on his trip to Hawaii instead of on *Beowulf*, taking an oral exam instead of the written one everyone else took, keeping the books for the annual instead of doing an accounting project.

Because the alternative assignments Alex managed to arrange were usually part of something he was already working on for some other purpose, he usually did well. Consequently his grades were quite good, though his SAT scores were mediocre. He charmed his way through his admissions interviews and was accepted to a prestigious private university. He registered as a marketing major in the College of Business and thought he was home free.

He wasn't. He discovered that everyone else in college was at least as smart as he was and that many were as charming. The hustles that had worked so well in high school were no longer successful. And the work was hard. He struggled to make Cs and was worried about his grades.

The social life, however, was terrific. For the first time in his life, Alex was part of a group of people who thought the way he did. Most of them lived in the same residence hall, most of them were business majors, and most of them really liked to have a good time. A few were involved in the college radio station. One night Alex sat in the booth while one of his new friends finished off his stint as disk jockey. Alex was hooked. Before long he had his own show on Sunday mornings: "Alex in the A.M." He could play all of his own favorite music; he could be as outrageous as he liked, and a few people actually listened.

By winter, Alex was living for the weekends. He would party with his pals on Friday nights, sleep most of Saturday, and then get ready for his Sunday morning show. Sunday afternoons he'd hang around with his friends talking about the station and moaning about how far behind he was in his classes.

He *was* far behind. When his friends were studying during the week, Alex was learning as much as he could about the contemporary music scene—research for his show. His grades suffered accordingly. At the end of the semester he received Cs in Introduction to Business and U.S. History, a D in Spanish, and an F in Accounting I. He was placed on probation.

His parents were gravely concerned. They told him that if he didn't raise his grades to at least a C average by the end of his freshman year, they were no longer going to pay for his college education. "You'd better drop this radio station nonsense," they said. "Probationary students have no time for extracurricular activities." Alex was depressed. He realized that he loved working in the radio station, and he wanted to do that sort of work for the rest of his life. In order to do that he needed more experience; where better than a college radio station? A degree would help as well, especially a degree in marketing.

The assistant dean who advised all probationary students counseled Alex to repeat Accounting I. The grade he received the second time around would replace the F on his transcript, instantly raising his GPA. And besides, he would need a solid background in accounting for any business major, even marketing. They agreed on College

Writing, Introduction to Mass Communications, and Earth Science I for the rest of Alex's spring schedule.

The assistant dean also advised Alex to stick with the radio station. "Everyone needs an interest outside of class," he said. "I see too many students who say they're going to study all of the time to get their grades up. Well, they don't. And before long they're not studying at all. In my experience, if you are responsible for something outside the classroom, your chances for succeeding are much better." He volunteered to speak to Alex's parents if they objected too strenuously.

Alex sought the help of his friends. Some of them had been quite successful in class, and all of them had done better than he had. How did they do it? They told him that they studied—*hard*—during the week so that they could mess around on weekends. They told him that they studied together for exams and that they helped each other on projects. They volunteered to tutor Alex in accounting; three of them had done well in the course. They set up a regular schedule: 4 P.M. on Monday, Wednesday, and Friday. Alex objected. "I like to take a nap in the afternoon, guys. And by 4 on Friday, I'm already at a party." They insisted; daily naps were out if he was really serious about improving his grades. And the Friday party could wait a little while.

Alex found studying difficult; he had never done much, after all. But his friends pushed him. They worked him hard for accounting: practice problems, drills on basic concepts, practice quizzes. He got a B+ on the first test and was absolutely delighted. His friends eased the pressure a little, and he received Bs thereafter. His parents and the assistant dean were pleased.

Writing papers was easy for Alex, if someone helped him get started. His roommate was in the same College Writing section; he offered to talk through the assignments with Alex, as long as they began the week before they were due. With his roommate's help, he received Bs and Cs on his papers.

Earth Science was a chore. The professor spoke in a monotone, the class was huge, the subject was boring, and it met at 8 A.M. in a room that was always too warm. Alex struggled to earn Cs. Mass Communications, on the other hand, was fun. They studied various media; Alex found newspapers and TV as fascinating as radio. They divided into groups to work on projects; Alex found that he could easily manipulate the group into following his ideas. For his final project, Alex and his group designed a marketing plan for the radio station. They received an A+, Alex earned an A− for the course, and the station hired him for the following year as Director of Marketing.

Alex still lives for the weekends. He starts partying a little later on Fridays, but otherwise he follows the same schedule as before. He has less time to research contemporary music because he spends at least a few hours studying most evenings during the week. Consequently he focuses his radio show on Latin American and Caribbean music, areas he already knows. With this focus, it has become quite popular. He is beginning to negotiate with a local radio station about an internship.

What saved Alex? For a time he looked doomed: too many parties, too much time spent with extracurricular activities, too little studying. But he turned his college career around. How?

First of all, he developed a genuine commitment to succeed. When he was in danger of washing out, he realized that he didn't want to fail—that he wanted to graduate with a degree in marketing. That commitment led him to do what he needed to do to succeed. Secondly, he developed his own definition of success. His parents told him that they wanted to see at least a C average; otherwise they would provide no more support. Raising his grades to a C average and staying active in the radio station became his goals for the second semester of his freshman year.

Third, Alex worked the system to his advantage. His college allows students to repeat failed courses and replace the F with the new grade; he did so. And he took advantage of his connections in the radio station to design an extremely successful final project for Mass Communications. Those connections will also help earn him an internship.

Fourth, Alex used his extracurricular activities to help, rather than hinder, his coursework. The radio station became his greatest interest; nothing was as much fun as talking on the radio. But he realized that he couldn't talk on the campus radio if he wasn't a student. So his passion for radio drove him to study—the only way he could remain a student. His experiences in the radio station also provided him with material for Mass Communications and for several papers for College Writing. And the increasing responsibility the station manager gave him increased his confidence in everything he tried.

Finally, Alex took advantage of his friends. Three business students offered to tutor him in accounting; he accepted their offer. His roommate offered to talk over paper assignments; Alex leapt at the opportunity. All of his pals served as his conscience during the week; he accepted their prodding. In doing so he discovered that learning collaboratively not only is productive, but can be less tedious than doing it all on your own.

Leandra

Leandra was a better-than-average student in high school. Her parents restricted her social life considerably, so she had a lot of available time. She spent most of it dreaming in front of the TV, but she studied enough to gain admission to the local state college. She enrolled as a chemistry major; she had done well in chemistry in high school, and her dad thought she might find work as a lab technician or a medical technologist after college.

College chemistry was different from high school chemistry. In high school if she could balance the equations describing reactions she was ahead of the game. In college she had to know a lot of detail, which required hard studying. She also had to spend long hours in the lab; if the experiment didn't work the first time, she had to come back at night and do it again. She made Cs on her lecture exams, but C minuses and Ds on her labs.

Freshman English was hard, also. Writing papers was not easy for Leandra, and she didn't like her instructor. She tried but couldn't seem to get her grades above C+. By Thanksgiving she wasn't trying as hard as she did at first. She wound up with a D for the course.

Introduction to Political Systems was strange. The professor had hair longer than hers and wore earrings. He seemed like some kind of radical; his lectures consisted of diatribes against the political systems they were studying. If anyone asked a question the professor would challenge the questioner's basic premises, rather than simply answering it. Leandra read everything he assigned but still got Ds on the exams. She just couldn't figure out what he wanted.

Algebra II was impossible. Leandra's dad had helped her get through high school math. He had wanted her to take calculus, but the math placement test at registration showed that she wasn't ready. The F she received in her first Algebra II exam convinced her that she wasn't ready for that, either. She dropped the course.

Leandra's only solace came from her friends. She and her roommate became good pals, and the two of them became close to two women in the next dorm. They spent all of their free time together. They went downtown nearly every afternoon, they watched TV together at night, they went out together on weekends. They started hanging around with four sophomores from the basketball team.

Leandra's three friends became her support group, her network. When she dropped algebra, they told her that she'd never need math anyway. They encouraged her to get a part-time job selling jeans in the mall. When she botched a chem experiment, they talked her into going out instead of repeating it. When her dad complained about her grades at midterm, they took her downtown to console her. When her new boyfriend dumped her, they arranged a blind date.

Leandra loved her new life. She was free to do whatever she wanted. Classes took up only a few hours a day. She could do her homework in an hour or two; if something came up, she could always do it later. Her social life in high school had been dull, dull, dull. But in college it was terrific. Her friends helped her learn how to drink, how to deal with men, how to get by on 5 hours of sleep. Life was great.

Except for her grades. At the end of the semester, Leandra earned a C in chemistry lecture and a D in lab, a D in Introduction to Political Systems, a D in Freshman English, and a Withdraw Failing in Algebra II. She didn't like it much, but her folks were furious. "Come home," they said. "We'll help you straighten out your life."

Leandra went home to visit but refused to stay. She told her folks that her life didn't need straightening out. "I like everything about going to college except the school part of it. I like my friends, I like being able to arrange my own schedule, I like my job. I just don't like going to class. So I'm dropping out. The store will hire me full time, and I'm going to share an apartment with a girl I know. We'll be fine."

And that's what she did. One of her pals dropped out also, and they found an affordable apartment downtown. The jeans store was delighted to hire her at the downtown store full time and encouraged her to think about applying to be assistant manager in a year or two. She reorganized her social life somewhat to fit her new schedule—working full time took up twice as many hours as she had ever spent on school—but there was still plenty of time left for being with her friends, dating, and generally hanging out. At the suggestion of her supervisor, she started investigating the fashion merchandising program at the local community college.

Is Leandra's story a tragedy? Not at all. True, she did not succeed in her courses. But going to college widened her horizons, helped her decide how she wanted to live her life, and led to a new definition of self. She may return someday, she may not. In either case, her semester at the university provided her with a good beginning.

Why didn't she succeed in her courses? First, the goals she was pursuing were invented for her by someone else—her father. Worthy goals, to be sure. But they had little to do with Leandra's capabilities or interests. Consequently they were difficult for her to pursue with any vigor.

Second, her extracurricular activities tended to pull her away from her schoolwork. She saw her social life, her job, her time with her friends as competition for her studies. Sometimes her studies would win the tug-of-war, sometimes her other activities would prevail. But she never came to see her life as an integrated whole, with its different parts complementing one another rather than competing, until she dropped out of school and went to work full time. Alex, by contrast, was able to make his radio activities contribute to his coursework.

Third, her friends did not contribute to her academic success. They helped her enormously in many ways; she would never have grown to be an independent person so quickly without them. But their interests were outside of the classroom, and they encouraged Leandra to look in the same directions.

Fourth, Leandra could never get beyond perceiving of school as a place where things are done to you. She saw no difference between her college political science teacher and her high school social studies teacher, even though the social studies teacher's method was designed to help students remember dates and the political scientist's method was designed to help students think. She saw no difference between her high school and college chemistry classes, even though her high school class was designed to meet the state science requirement and the college class was designed to prepare students for careers in the health professions. To Leandra, nothing that happened in her classes had any relevance to her life. Consequently she never felt a part of the place.

When she took control of her life by dropping out of school and going to work, she began to see her environment as one she had created for herself—at least in part. Her job, her living situation, and her social life were her own constructions. If she returns to school, her academic life will be her own construction as well. She will do well.

There's nothing wrong with making fun your number one priority. Many people live happy, productive, admirable lives pursuing a good time. They have realized what their goals are, and they do whatever they must to reach them. Alex followed that pattern, eventually. His first semester, he floundered about. But in the shock of doing poorly he found a new goal: a career in radio. He needed to stay in school and to earn a degree in marketing in order to reach his goal. Consequently he pushed himself in his courses and succeeded.

Leandra, on the other hand, never connected her coursework with any personal goals. Fun with her friends was her number one priority. She learned quickly that she could pursue her priority by giving up school altogether. She may eventually succeed at college, but only if she sees the courses she takes as contributing to her own aims.

EXERCISE 13.1

Do you know any students like Alex or Leandra? Will they succeed? Why or why not? How are you different from them? Write your answers in your journal.

14

The Athletes

Some students think of going to college as a vehicle for athletics. That's not surprising; the earliest introduction most of us have to college is college athletics on television: the Rose Bowl, the NCAA basketball tournament, the innumerable swimming meets and gymnastics competitions and wrestling tournaments that are on cable TV around the clock. And some students are more successful in athletics than anything else in high school; why should they expect anything different in college?

Because college is different from high school.

Aaron

Aaron grew up in the inner city, in a housing project. He was blessed with tall parents; he reached 6'4" by his sophomore year in high school. By then he was starting forward on the basketball team at Central High. He made the conference all-star team as a junior and all-state as a senior. Heavily recruited for his basketball talents, he accepted a full-ride scholarship (based on both need and his athletic promise) at State U, the giant public university 100 miles away.

Aaron's grades in high school were good enough for admission to State—3.1 on a 4.0 scale, about 70th percentile in his graduating class. His teachers and coaches all thought the world of him and predicted great things. His ambition was to play college ball and major in premed, then—if he was good enough— play in the NBA for a few years before going to medical school.

State offered him a place in a summer precollege program for low-income minority students. He turned it down; the basketball coach wanted him to spend the summer in the weight room bulking up. So he stayed home, worked out afternoons at Central, and worked nights at the Quick-Stop. He reported to campus at the end of August, ready to be a hero.

The problem was that Aaron was black, and nearly everyone else was white. Further, he was a black athlete—doubly special. Everyone looked at him, and when they asked if he were a basketball player, he had to confess that he was. All of the other freshmen could be whatever they wanted—smart or dumb, social or antisocial, Greek or independent, partiers or grinds. He was stuck being a black basketball player.

The Housing Office assigned him to a residence hall for athletes. He didn't dislike it; he'd been hanging around jocks all of his life. But no one there studied much, except in the mandatory study halls run by grad students hired by the coaching staff. It seemed more like high school than college. The bull sessions were mostly devoted to sports, and they didn't last long—11 o'clock curfew. His high school English teacher had told him about arguments on music, politics, and ideas lasting until dawn. He missed that.

The athlete's academic adviser scheduled him into Remedial Math, Remedial English, Principles of Photography, and History of the American West, and told him to drop history after a few weeks. Athletes have to start with 12 credits, she said, but they only have to finish with 9. "Where's my premed course?" he asked. She told him that premed might be a problem for a full-time athlete at State because the coaches expected lots of practice time. But he could trade his history course for Biology 151, the first step in the premed sequence, if he wanted. "Don't forget," she told him, "you can drop it without penalty during the first half of the semester, and you'll still be a full-time student."

Bio 151 was competitive: sixty freshmen, all desperate for the As that would keep them on track for med school. They studied all of the time. They formed study groups. They all seemed to know one another. And they looked at Aaron as if he were from another planet. The only other blacks were women, and they treated him as if he were—well, as if he were a basketball player. Still, he managed to keep up during the first month. He even earned a B− on the first exam. His other courses were cake.

Then practice started. Suddenly he had to spend 3 hours each afternoon in the gym, an hour each night in meetings, an hour every other day in the weight room, and odd minutes here and there learning plays. Weekends were for scrimmages until the season started; then the team would play every Thursday and Saturday night. No one seemed to study much, except in study hall—where most of the athletes studied their play books.

Aaron got in trouble with the coach on the second day of practice. He was 5 minutes late; he'd had to wait for the biology lab instructor to check over the cat he was dissecting. Coach cut his explanation short. "Don't give me that bio lab crap, I've heard it all before. You boys think you're hot stuff, high school heroes, city league all-stars, playground champs. Around here you'll do it my way or lose your scholarship. That means being at practice on time."

He could handle being yelled at. All coaches sound pretty much the same, and he knew they were just making an example of him for the other players. But he didn't like being called "boy," and he didn't like coach implying that all black players were prima donnas. Most of all, he didn't like having to leave his biology lab early to make it to practice. His most successful classmates hung around for a few minutes to review what they had done with the lab instructor.

Things got worse. In order to have enough time to study his biology, he started cutting his other courses. They were easy for him, after all. And why spend time in remedial classes, which weren't going to count toward a premed degree? The athletic department's academic adviser caught him after study hall one night and told him that if he cut any more classes, his spot on the team would be in jeopardy; the department had a strict rule about class attendance. So he went back to class, and let some of his biology slide.

In high school, basketball was relaxing. Not at State. "Basketball is your job," coach would say. "In order to succeed at your job, you have to work at it all the time." Aaron worked at it, but everybody was bigger, stronger, and faster than anyone else he had ever played with or against. It was hard work just to keep up. The assistant coaches were always on him: "Crank it up another notch, Aaron; you've got to spend more time in the weight room, Aaron; we need a total commitment from you, Aaron."

His social life was easy; there was none. Basketball, classes, and studying biology took all of his time. The only black women he knew were premed grinds. Some of the other women liked to hang around athletes, but he didn't like being treated like an exotic animal. Once practice started he couldn't even go home for an occasional weekend. The most fun he had was when the black ballplayers got together to give each other haircuts.

By the end of the semester he was in serious trouble. He scraped through biology with a C− and earned Cs in his other courses. (His adviser called them "jock Cs," with a smirk.) On the court he was hanging on, but not doing well. Coach told him that he wouldn't play much this season, but they had hopes for the future. "Keep up the weights, commit yourself to basketball, and you'll do fine." He had no friends, no place to go to relax, no joy in his life. He hated it.

He talked to his mom about dropping out. "Don't do it," she said. "Remember what you used to say—quitters never win, winners never quit. Maybe you have to choose: basketball or premed." But which? Being a doctor had always been his dream. But basketball was real; most of his successes had come on the court, and he had confidence in his ability to keep succeeding as a ballplayer. Who knew if he could make it in medicine?

So he went back to State for second semester, registered for all of the courses the athletic adviser recommended, and committed himself to improving at basketball. It didn't work. His courses were so boring he could barely stand to go to class. He did no better on the court than he had first semester. And he still had no joy in his life.

At the end of the year he told the coaches he wanted to take some time off to figure out what he would do with his life; would they hold his scholarship? "Nope. Rule against it. Sorry you couldn't cut it, Aaron. But lots of boys can't commit as much as we require; don't let it get you down. Let us know how things turn out for you, hear?"

Aaron spent the next year working as many hours as he could at the Quick-Stop. When he wasn't working he was playing ball, either in the high school gym or in the playgrounds, or hanging out with his friends. He wouldn't talk about his year at State; "it just didn't work out," he would say when asked.

In May the high school coach caught him in the gym and asked him what he was doing with his life. "Not much." "Why don't you think about the community college downtown? They have a strong academic program—you wanted to be premed, right? At least you could get into a med tech program. And you could still play ball." "Will they give me a scholarship?" "No, but you don't need an athletic scholarship. Financial aid will pay your tuition, and you can live at home."

Aaron registered the following fall. He signed up for Freshman Composition, Calculus I, Chemistry I, and Introduction to Sociology. They accepted his credits for Biology 151, but for none of the other courses he had taken at State. "Sorry; we don't transfer anything less than a C, and most of these courses are remedial or not offered here."

He told his adviser he wanted to play basketball, but only for fun. "No problem," he said; "athletics are not taken very seriously here." And the coach agreed. "School comes first. Try and schedule your labs around practice times, but we'll work something out."

Best of all, at the community college he wasn't unusual. A good third of the students were persons of color: black, Hispanic, Asian, even a few Native Americans. They didn't give him a second look, and no one seemed to care if he was an athlete or not. He felt at home.

From the first day, his classes went well. He was well prepared for English, after two remedial courses at State, so that didn't take much time. Sociology was interesting, and he could read enough on the bus to make Bs. Aaron devoted most of his study time to calculus and chemistry. It paid off; he earned an A and a B.

Basketball was, well, basketball. He went to practice late 2 days a week so he could go to a tutoring session in calculus; the coach accepted his explanation and never complained. He began the season as sixth man and was starting by the end. He played well, enjoyed it, and was able to put basketball out of his mind when he wasn't playing.

Aaron's social life was still nonexistent. He worked weekends to help his folks with the rent and spent evenings studying. But he didn't feel like a misfit any more. He felt like a student.

After 2 successful years at the community college, Aaron transferred back to State. But not as a basketball player—as a biology major headed for medical school. He brought a solid 3.2 GPA and all of the required courses, and he was accepted without question—and without reference to his athletic prowess. State awarded him a chancellor's scholarship for high-ability minority students. He played intramural basketball when he had time.

Last year Aaron began his first year at State's medical school. He is working very hard and managing to keep up. He has started having coffee with one of the women from his study group; he thinks they might go out soon. Basketball is limited to late-night pickup games; he and his friends find it relaxing.

Aaron's first year at State was not a success. But it wasn't a total loss, either. He learned that basketball was not the most important part of his life. And he learned that his own goals did not match the goals his athletic and academic advisers had set for him. He wanted to be a student; everyone around him wanted him to be an athlete. Aaron was a misfit.

Dropping out was a very wise move, as it turned out. In the community college his goals fit perfectly. His instructors, coaches, and classmates were willing to accept his own definition of himself: a student who plays ball. By the time he returned to State, Aaron's self-definition was secure.

Suzy

Suzy grew up in the suburbs, the only child of a sports-minded couple. Dad competed in football and baseball in high school and college and still plays softball in neighborhood leagues. Mom would have competed if there had been an opportunity, but she went to school before Title IX opened the doors for women in athletics. She settled for being a cheerleader. Suzy was encouraged to participate in sports from the time she could walk.

In high school she played volleyball, basketball, and softball. She did well in all three, but volleyball was her favorite. She made all-conference as a junior and all-state in her senior year. At the Senior All-Sports Banquet she was named to the school's athletic hall of fame.

As a student Suzy was bright, cooperative, and industrious, but she never could earn grades better than average. Her teachers always said it was because she spent so much time on athletics. Her parents were happy to believe it; they valued success in sports more than good grades anyway. As long as she was keeping up in the classroom, they were satisfied.

Suzy planned to go into business, as her dad had done. She was recruited by the volleyball coach at a medium-sized public university in a neighboring state, one that had recently been selling itself as a "public ivy; get an ivy league education at a public school price." Her own state university offered her a volleyball scholarship, but she was worried about the size of the place. Besides, her dad liked the prestige of the public ivy and was easily able to pay the costs. So she went.

At first Suzy liked everything about college. The size was manageable; it had just a few thousand students, so she wasn't overwhelmed.

The people were all friendly, and her roommate—a sophomore volleyball player—was great. Freshman orientation was a little boring, but okay. She even liked the food. Her classes were mostly interesting. Freshman Rhetoric, a speech and writing course, was in many ways similar to the speech class she had loved in high school. Introduction to American Business was okay; the instructor was boring, but at least she could relate it to some of the history of the company her dad owned. College Algebra was tough, but she thought she could handle it. And it was a prerequisite for calculus, which was required of all business majors. At the suggestion of her adviser she had signed up for a 1-credit freshman seminar, The Culture of the Sixties. She loved it; she'd heard her folks talk wistfully about growing up during the Sixties all of her life.

Volleyball went well from the beginning. By the third match she was starting; her coach was predicting great things of her. Her classes did not go nearly so well. In Rhetoric, the tests and quizzes were bearable; Cs and C pluses. The talk she gave in class ("Learning Through Sports") earned an A. But her papers were coming back with Ds and D minuses. Algebra was tougher than she had thought, but she was managing to earn Cs. The freshman seminar was fun—they listened to music a lot—but the reading seemed overwhelming, especially for a 1-credit course.

Suzy's high school coach had warned her that college would be different from high school; success in athletics would not count as much. She was finding that to be true. Her teammates liked and respected her, and that was great. But no one else on campus paid any attention. The students stayed away from volleyball matches in droves, and the instructors didn't even know there was a team. She found herself missing home, and high school, more and more.

After midterm exams (C− in Rhetoric, D in Intro to Business, C in Algebra, F in the freshman seminar), Suzy's rhetoric instructor took her aside. "Have you ever been tested for dyslexia?" she asked. Suzy had never even heard of it. "Dyslexia is a learning disability. It causes reading and writing problems; no one knows exactly how, but apparently dyslexic persons mix up the letters they see on the page. So reading is a problem, and spelling is very difficult. I've noticed that your spelling is atrocious, and you seem to be a slow reader."

"Spelling is a knack I never had; my dad can't spell either. And I've never liked to read. Unless it's about sports."

Suzy didn't like to think that she might have a disability. On the other hand, maybe dyslexia would explain the problems she was having in class. So she went off to the Counseling Center to be tested. After batteries of tests, the counselor concluded that she was, indeed, mildly dyslexic—but that she had developed strategies on her own to help her cope. She could read adequately, though slowly. Writing was difficult, however. She could not spell, and organizing a paper was hard; hence her paper grades in Freshman Rhetoric.

In high school, Suzy's verbal skills had helped to make up for her writing deficiencies. And her success in athletics had more than made up for her average grades, in the eyes of her friends and her parents. But in college, no one was very impressed by her prowess on the volleyball court. The counselor saw the dismay on her face. "It's not going to get any worse," she said. "And learning disabilities are not contagious; you can't give it to your roommate."

"You don't understand. Nobody understands. My classes are going to hell, nobody likes me, and I miss my dad." The counselor could see that dyslexia was not the only problem facing Suzy. She talked to her for half an hour on the spot and suggested a regular weekly session thereafter. Suzy was resistant. "I'm not crazy. What do I need a counselor for?" "Counselors can help all sorts of students, Suzy. Going to college is hard; lots of students have temporary problems, just as you do. Counseling can help you solve them; why not give it a try?"

Suzy found that counseling was very helpful. She had been used to getting lots of uncritical support from her folks and her friends. But they were hundreds of miles away. And her new friends, though they liked her fine, didn't treat her quite like the heroine she had been in high school. Faye, the counselor, supported her as uncritically as her parents did.

Their first task was to deal with Suzy's learning disability. Faye introduced her to the learning disabilities specialist at the Academic Assistance Center. Suzy learned that there is no cure for dyslexia, but that there are various ways to alter one's behavior to accommodate it. Her case was quite mild; she could read, though slowly, and write, though poorly. The specialist prescribed a computer for writing.

"No one quite knows why, but learning-disabled students who write their papers on computers do much better than if they write longhand or even on a typewriter. Maybe the computer's capacity to make corrections painlessly is liberating. Maybe being able to see your work on the screen helps you see your mistakes. Maybe it's just the automatic spell-checker. Who cares? It works." And it did work. At first Suzy used the computers in the Academic Assistance Center. She had learned to type in high school, but she had never used a computer to write a paper before. She found it wonderful. She could start by brainstorming ideas, just as her rhetoric instructor recommended. Once she had decided what to say, she could write a short outline, expand it, change around the major points as she felt like it, and even change her mind. Once she had an outline on the screen, writing the paper was almost as easy as filling in the blanks. And the spell-checker fixed most of her spelling mistakes. Suddenly she was getting Bs on her papers. She quickly talked her dad into buying her a personal computer and printer. Having them in her dormitory room made writing even easier.

The specialist could not help her quite so quickly with reading. "You've already done the hard part: figuring out how to decode written language. It just takes you a little while longer than most people. Try the exercises in this book; they'll help you read a little faster. And practice a lot. You've never read much, right? That's probably most of the problem. But listen: If you ever have a text that is just incomprehensible, let me know and we'll get you a reader." The book the specialist lent her also contained some reading techniques: skimming and scanning, reading for the main idea, and so on.

The exercises helped a little. She found that the reading techniques were especially helpful with the lengthy readings for her freshman seminar. She managed to raise her grade in that course to a C by the end of the quarter. She carried her Cs in Intro to Business and Algebra; in Rhetoric, a B. She was quite proud of herself. Her dad asked her what made the difference—she'd been so down on herself at midterm. "Well, the Academic Assistance Center helped a lot. That computer's great, Dad; thanks for sending it to me. (By the way, have you ever been tested for a learning disability?) But, more than anything else, it was Faye, my counselor. She helped me see that I could succeed in college, that I was more than just a volleyball star. She's really great; I'm going to keep seeing her the rest of this year."

What happened here? Suzy floundered a bit early, thought she was failing, and then caught herself before the end of the quarter. How did she do it?

Primarily through the intervention of the Counseling Center. Her major difficulty was the loss of her source of self-esteem. In high school she was known primarily as an athlete. But in college women's athletics don't get much attention. Her friends and instructors regarded volleyball as a mildly interesting pastime, on a par with stamp collecting or frisbee golf. Faye helped her understand that volleyball was not the extent of her world, that there are other areas in which she could succeed and earn respect.

Suzy also suffered from a mild learning disability. She had learned to accommodate her disability, to a degree, but she needed assistance —especially with writing. She received that assistance from the Academic Assistance Center in time to make a difference in her first quarter—and in time to help rebuild her self-esteem before she failed completely.

What lessons can you learn from Aaron and Suzy? If you are an athlete, you should learn that athletics are not quite as important in college as in high school. If athletics are your focus, you will probably be disappointed by college. (Of course, there are exceptions. Colleges and universities are prone to worshipping athletes, just as high schools are—and just as our society is. But the level of competition is so much higher at the college level that very few high school stars become college stars.)

What can you do about that? Broaden your focus. Find some other areas in which you can succeed. Most colleges will be delighted to help you do that. A few, such as the giant state university that recruited Aaron solely as a basketball player, will not. But even at those schools, you can choose to define yourself as something other than an athlete, as Aaron eventually did.

Both Aaron and Suzy profited from the support systems their schools provided. Suzy received excellent counseling from the Counseling Center and crucial assistance from the Academic Assistance Center. Aaron got accurate, though limited, advice from the athletic department's academic adviser at State and good support from a variety of folks at the Community College.

Finally, both Aaron and Suzy learned that athletics, for almost all students, are for fun. A few—a very few—student athletes are talented and driven enough to make a career out of athletics. But remember that there are over 3,000 colleges and universities in this country. Virtually all of them support athletics at some level. But only a few hundred schools support athletics at the highest level—the level that gives athletic scholarships—and only a handful of student athletes, most of them from those few hundred schools, can make a living at athletics after they leave college. For the remaining 99.9 percent of college athletes, athletics are a sideline. They provide exercise, a release for competitive urges, something to think about besides classes, social contact, and fun.

What part do athletics play in your life? Are you a participant? At what level (intercollegiate, intramurals, pickup)? Are you a fan?

If athletics play any part in your life, why? Is that part appropriate? What can you learn from athletics, either from participating or from being a fan?

CHAPTER 15

Conclusion

The case studies of Part III demonstrate that succeeding in college is not easy. Expectations are high, pressures can be intense, and the work is frequently difficult. The preface to this book told you that you can succeed in college; I hope you have convinced yourself of that by now.

First of all, you must know why you are going to college. Without a set of goals—even tentative goals—you are lost. (I went to college for 2 years without any real goals. I wound up on probation and dropped out for a year. When I returned I knew that I wanted to graduate, at least—I had learned what life was like without an education. That was enough of a goal to earn me a degree and a fellowship to graduate school.)

Second, you must either possess or develop the skills you need, whatever they might be: skills in doing math, writing, talking to professors, organizing your time, dealing with your peers, seeking assistance when you need it. No one brings all of these skills to college—what more would you expect to learn? Everyone must develop at least some of them. Identify the skills that you need and do whatever you must to develop them.

Third, you have to use all of the resources at your disposal. Use the skills and experiences you bring with you. Use whatever help your family and friends can provide. Use all of the services your college offers you.

Finally, you have to engage yourself in the task. You can't treat college the way most of us treated high school—as a place where people do things to you for a few hours every day. Going to college should take at least a large part of your attention, even if you are a part-time student. Remember that what you do outside of class is relevant to your course work and that your coursework is relevant to your life.

Tie together what you have learned about yourself and college by completing this exercise.

FINAL EXERCISE

In your journal, write your own story. What sort of student were you when you entered college? What were your goals? What sorts of difficulties have you run into as you have pursued them? Where have you found help?

Will you succeed? How? Will you have to change your behavior in order to reach your goals? What will you do first?

This is a good exercise to repeat every 6 months or so. You will find that your perception of yourself changes, your goals change, your definition of success changes. Writing this exercise will help you recognize those changes and incorporate them into your life.

Enjoy your journey.

Index

notebooks. *See* journals; loose-
leaf notebooks; spiral-
bound notebooks
notes
adding supplemental
material to, 111–12
borrowing, 39–40
notes on, 99
reviewing, 85, 99
note taking
Cornell method, 107–10
in lectures, 95, 97, 98–102
outline method, 104–6, 107
reading and, 126–29
shorthand in, 101–2, 103
write-it-all-down method,
103–4, 105

outlining
of lecture notes, 104–6, 107
of reading notes, 126–27

pencils
reading with, 116–17
reviewing lecture notes with,
99
as study aid, 40
practice tests
for foreign language courses,
161
math, 155–56
as review technique, 88
study groups and, 67
prereading, 117–18
primacy effect, 86, 87
professors
cultivating good relations
with, 7–8, 11
expectations of, 29
internships and, 143
research projects with, 52–53
socializing with, 50

reading, 115–16
active, 116, 119
adjusting style of, 118–19
integrating notes with lecture notes, 129–30
for main idea, 123–24
math texts, 152–54
note taking and, 119, 126–29
preparing for, 117–18
scanning for answers, 124–25
SQ3R method of, 120–21
techniques for, 118–25
3R method of, 121–23
recency effect, 86, 87
recitation
of lecture notes, 108
of reading notes, 120, 121–22
relationships, 57–59
repetition, and remembering,
38–39, 44, 78–80, 84–85
research
collaborative, 69–70
for professors, 52–53
returning adults
involvement of, in co- and
extracurricular activi-
ties, 48
jobs vs. schoolwork and,
55–56
learning centers for, 51
motivations of, 4–5
time management by, 13–14
reviewing
lecture notes, 85, 99, 130
math, 155–57
reading notes, 85, 119, 121,
130
in study groups, 66–68, 87–
88, 154–55
review sessions, 50, 85
roommates, getting along with,
58

scanning, for answers, 124–25
schedules
   advantages and disadvan-
      tages of, 26–27
   daily, 23–24
   examples of, 16–18, 24
   quarter/semester, 25
   revising, 22–23
   weekly, 14–23
sensory memory, 74
sex, 58–59*n*
shorthand, in note taking,
   101–2, 103
short-term memory, 74
signal words, in lectures,
   100–101
socializing, with professors, 50
speaking, and learning, 43–45
spiral-bound notebooks
   for journals, 6, 41
   for lecture notes, 99, 108, 111
splitters, 35–37, 66
SQ3R reading technique,
   120–21
stress
   management of, 22
   reducing via exercise, 60
study abroad, 53
study groups
   collaborative learning in,
      66–68
   exam preparation and,
      87–88
   for math courses, 154–55

studying
   best times for, 19–20
   for exams, 85–89
   two-for-one rule of, 19
   writing and, 39–41
syllabus
   planning from, 30, 32–33
   sample, 31–32
   types of, 30, 33

tests. *See* exams
3R reading technique, 121–22
time management
   daily schedules, 23–24
   importance of, 13–14
   quarter/semester schedules,
      25
   weekly schedules, 14–23
tutoring
   collaborative, 70–71
   in learning centers, 51–52
two-for-one rule, 19

underlining, 116, 117, 121, 126

word processors, 159–60
work–study programs, 55
writing
   collaborative, 68–69
   importance of, in course-
      work, 39–43
   practice, 158–59
   about reading, 119
   word processors and, 159–60